EASY PIANO

FIRST 50 CLASSIC ROCK SONGS
YOU SHOULD PLAY ON THE PIANO

Simply arranged, must-know collection of classic rock favorites!

T0066480

ISBN 978-1-4950-7418-9

7777 W. BLUEMOUND RD. P.O. BOX 13819 MILWAUKEE, WI 53213

Visit Hal Leonard Online at
www.halleonard.com

CONTENTS

AFRICA

Words and Music by DAVID PAICH
and JEFF PORCARO

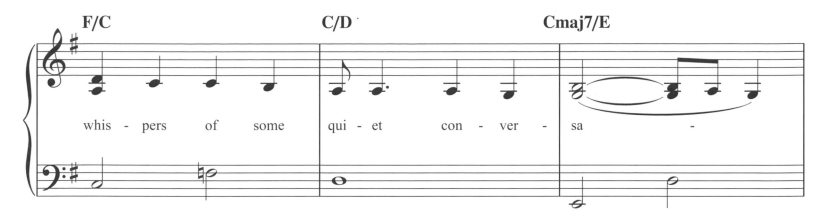

whis - pers of some qui - et con - ver - sa -

tion.

She's com - ing
The wild dogs

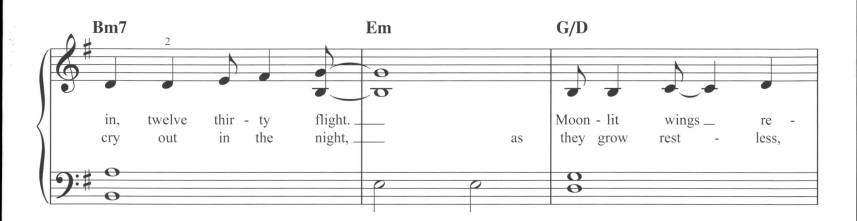

in, twelve thir - ty flight. ___
cry out in the night, ___ as

Moon - lit wings ___ re -
they grow rest - less,

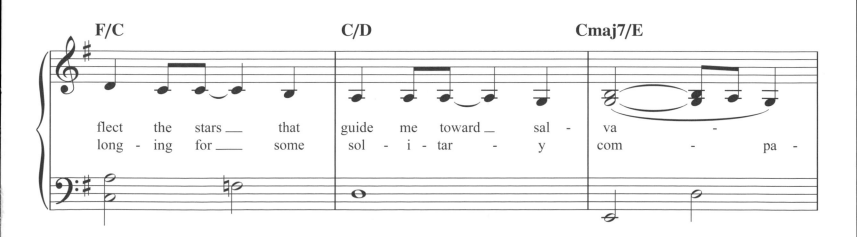

flect the stars ___ that guide me toward ___ sal - va -
long - ing for ___ some sol - i - tar - y com - pa -

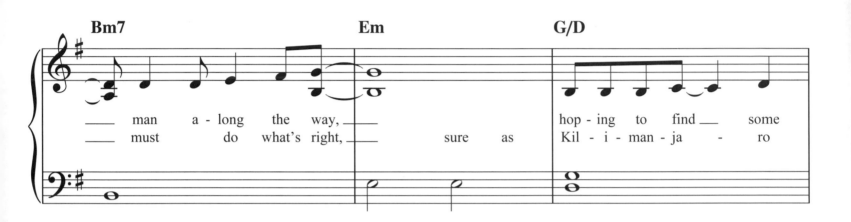

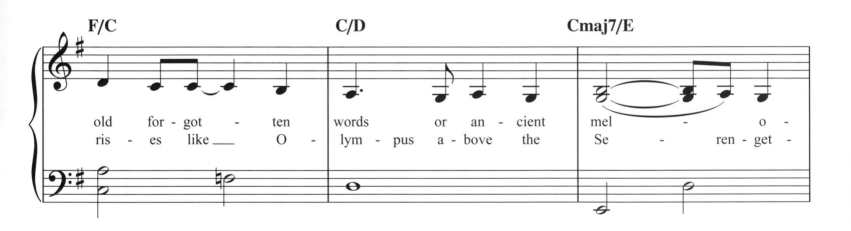

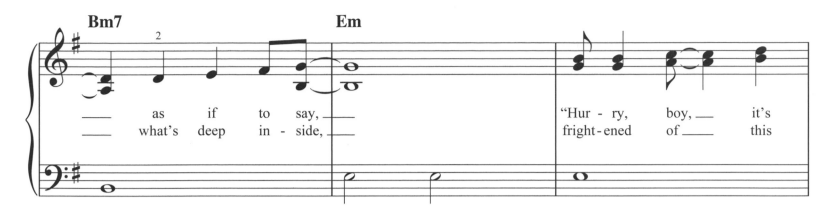

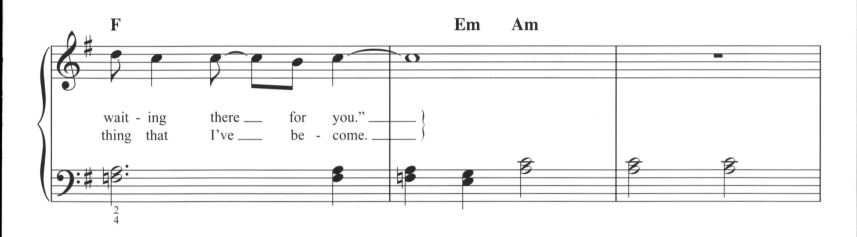

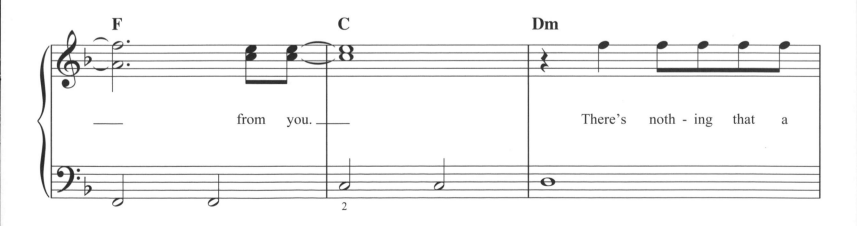

hun - dred   men ___   or   more ___   could   ev - er   do. ___

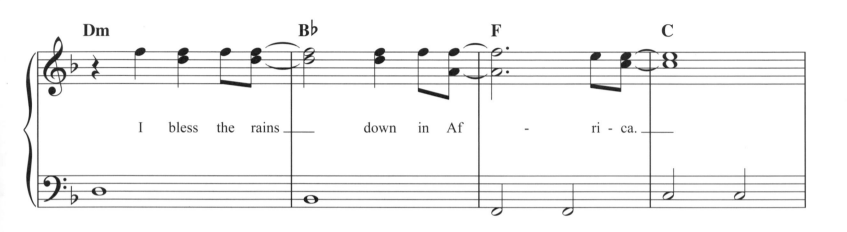

I   bless   the   rains ___   down   in   Af   -   ri - ca. ___

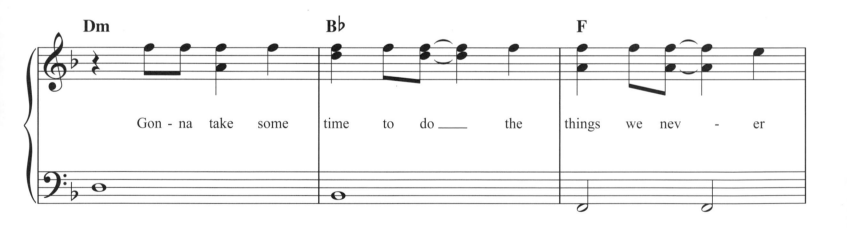

Gon - na   take   some   time   to   do ___   the   things   we   nev   -   er

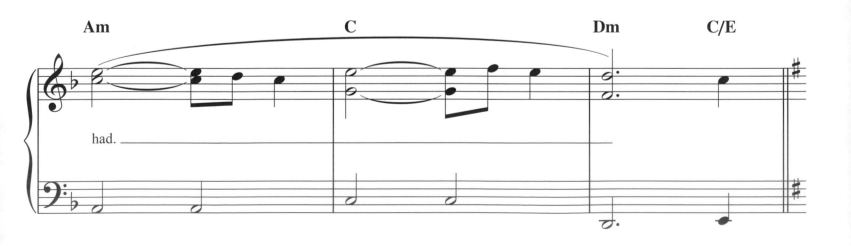

had. _____

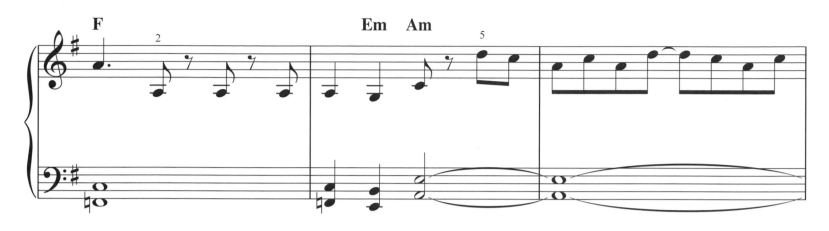

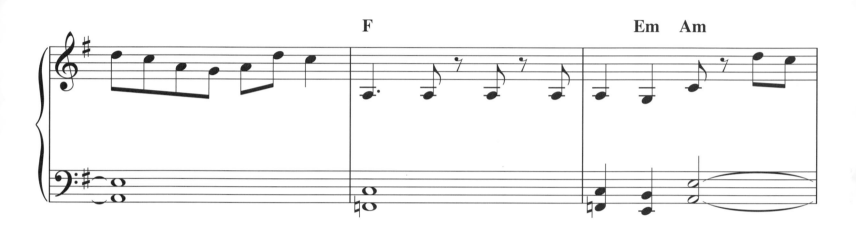

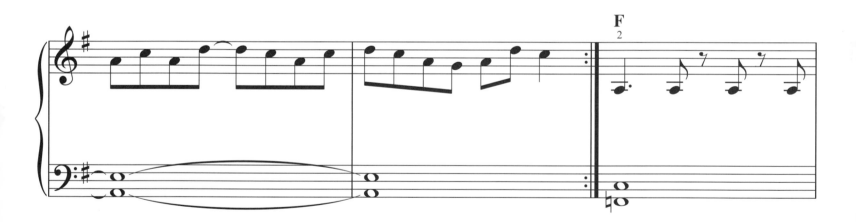

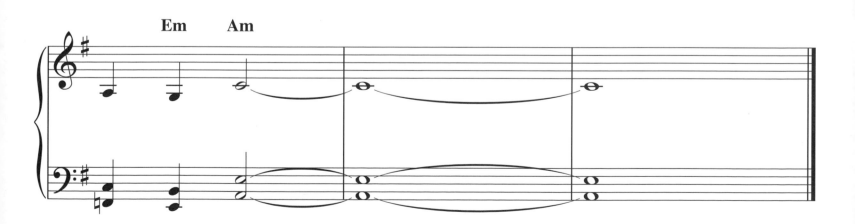

ANGIE

Words and Music by MICK JAGGER
and KEITH RICHARDS

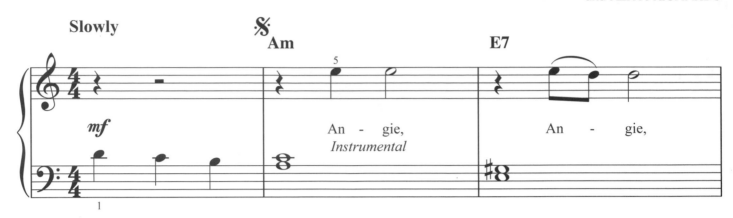

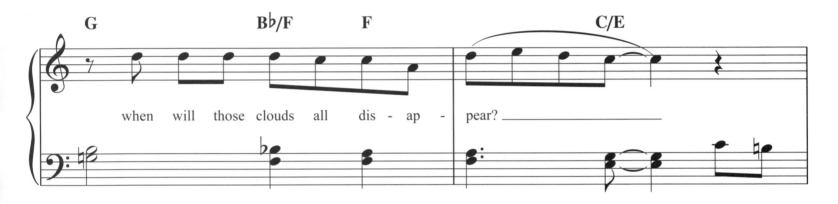

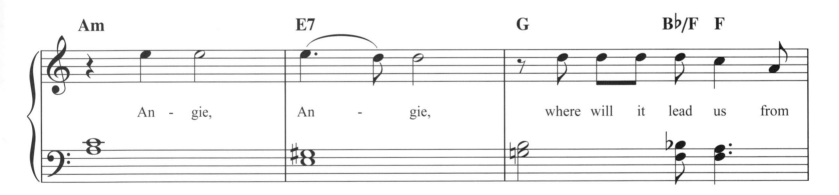

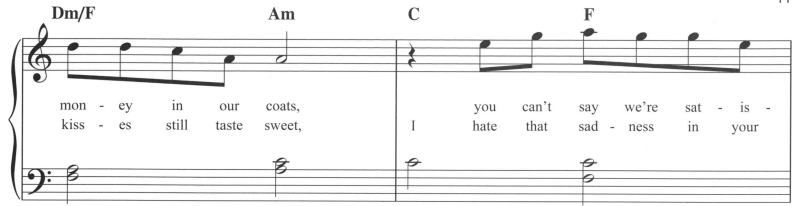

mon - ey in our coats,
kiss - es still taste sweet,

you can't say we're sat - is -
I hate that sad - ness in your

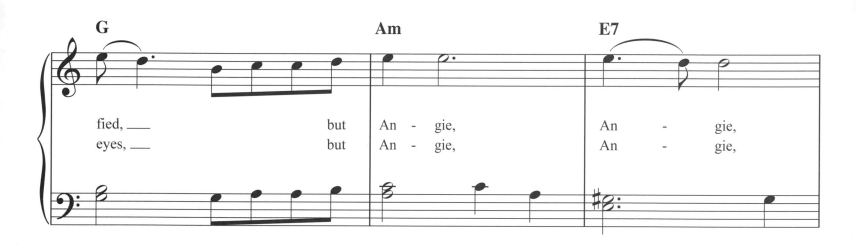

fied, ___ but An - gie,
eyes, ___ but An - gie,

An - gie,
An - gie,

you can't say we nev - er
ain't it time we said good -

tried. ___
bye? ___

(Oh, ___

To Coda ⊕

An - gie, you're beau - ti - ful,
yes.) *Instrumental*

but ain't it time we said good -

bye? _____

An - gie,

I still love you,

re - mem - ber all those nights we

cried? _____ All the

dreams we held so close seemed to

all go up in smoke,

let me whis - per in your

ear; _____

"An - gie,

An - gie,

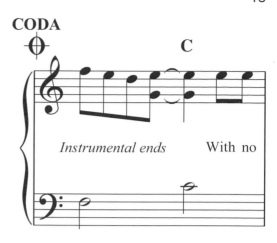

D.S. al Coda

CODA

where will it lead us from here?" _____

Instrumental ends With no

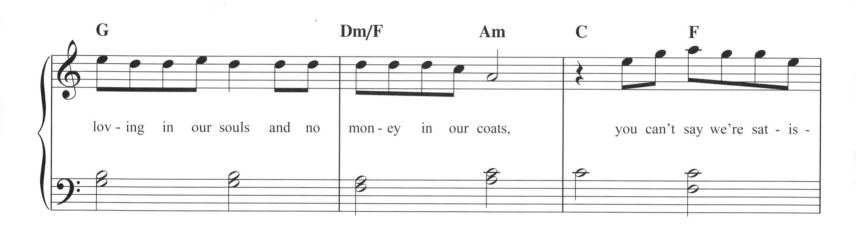

lov - ing in our souls and no mon - ey in our coats, you can't say we're sat - is -

fied, ___ but An - gie, I still love you, ba - by,

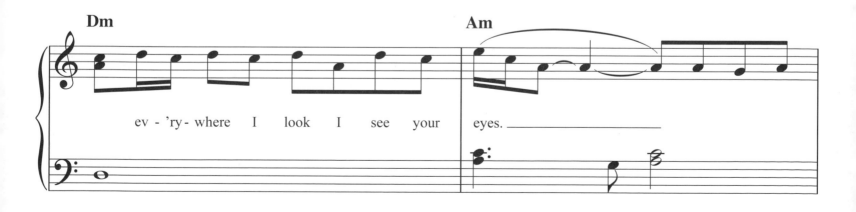

ev - 'ry - where I look I see your eyes. _____

CHANGES

Words and Music by
DAVID BOWIE

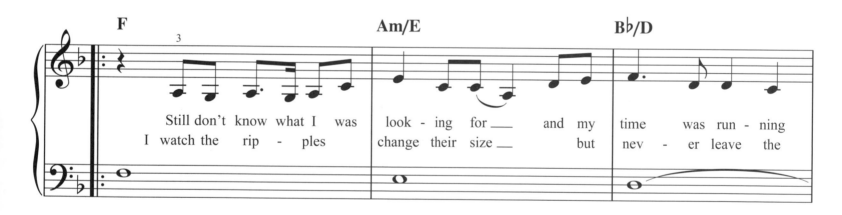

Still don't know what I was look-ing for ___ and my time was run-ning
I watch the rip-ples change their size ___ but nev-er leave the

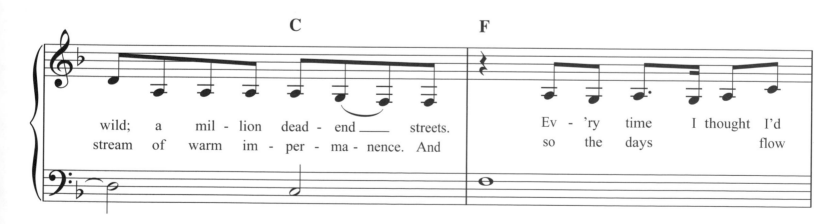

wild; a mil-lion dead-end ___ streets.   Ev-'ry time I thought I'd
stream of warm im-per-ma-nence. And   so the days flow

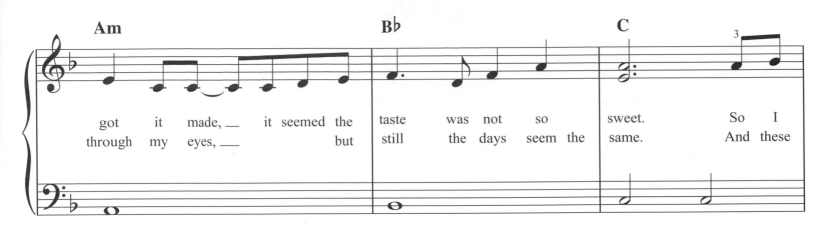

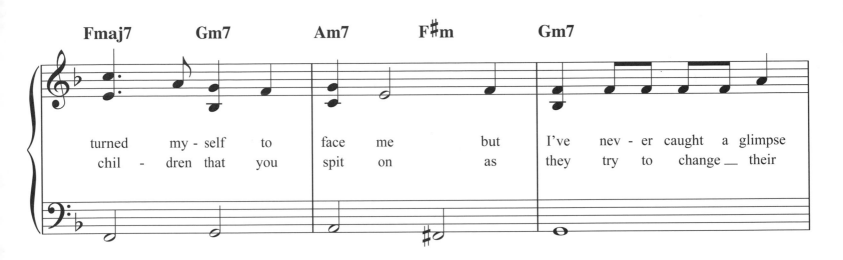

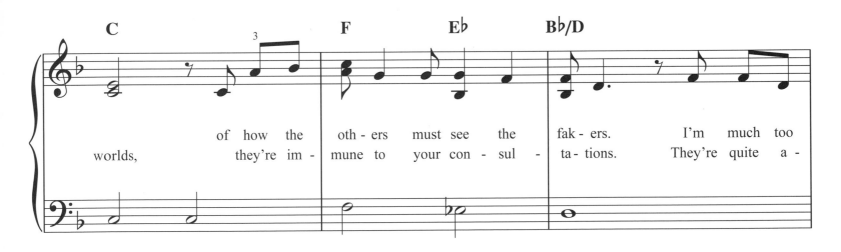

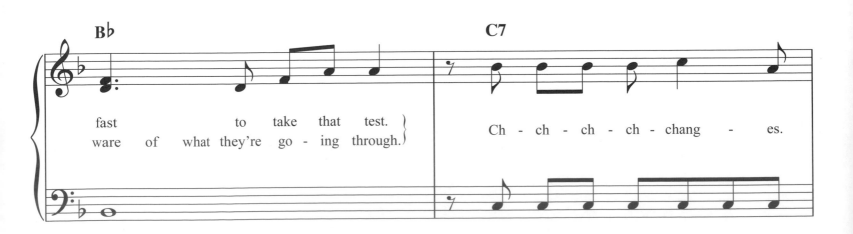

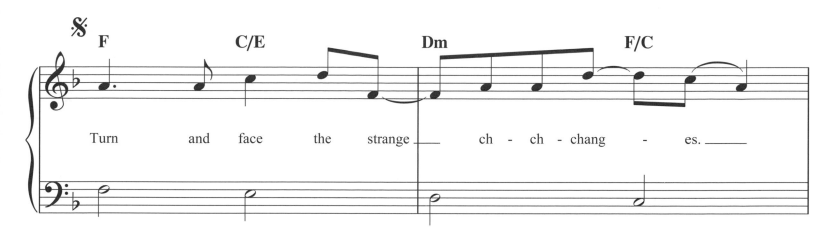

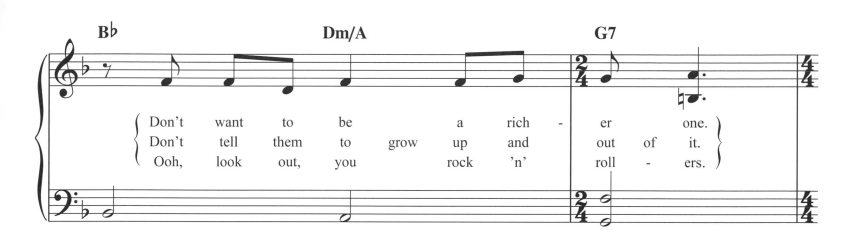

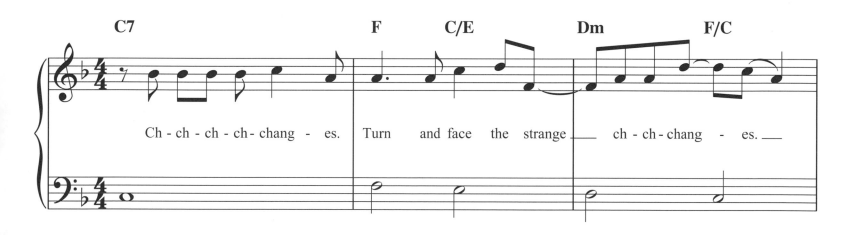

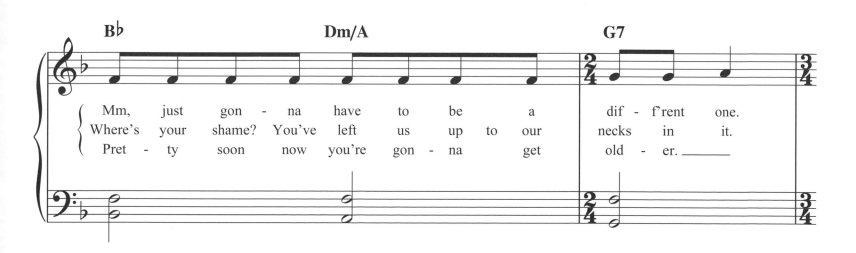

To Coda

Time may change me, but I can't trace
Time may change me, but you can't trace
Time may change me, but I can't trace

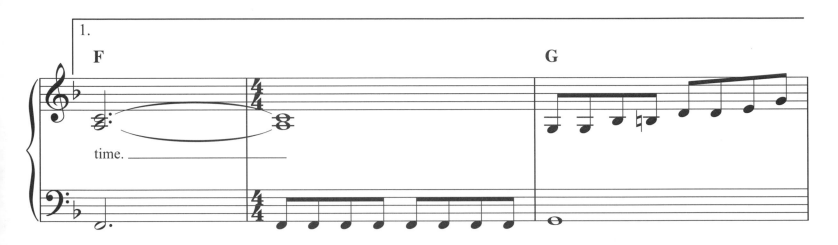

time.

time.

Strange fas - ci - na - tion, ___ fas -

'nat - ing me. ____ Ah, ____ chang - es ____ are

tak - ing ____ the pace I'm go - ing through. Ch - ch - ch - ch - chang - es.

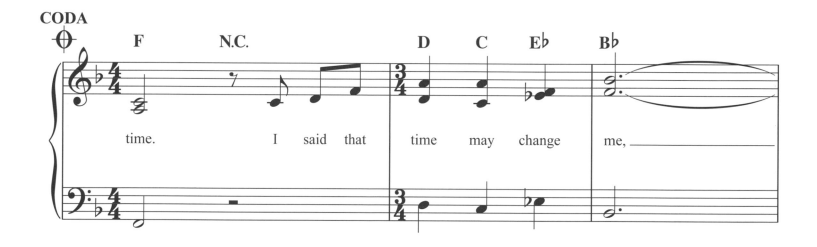

time. I said that time may change me, ____

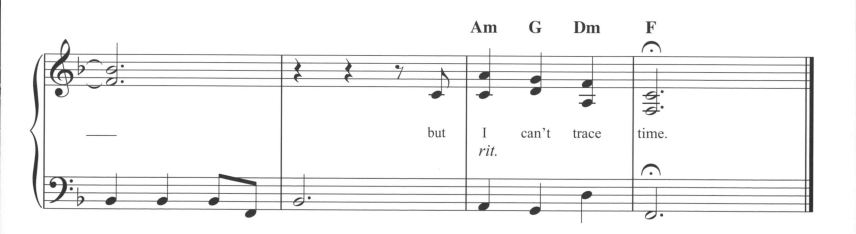

____ but I can't trace time.

BEHIND BLUE EYES

Words and Music by
PETE TOWNSHEND

No one knows what it's like to be the bad man,
No one knows what it's like to feel these feel - ings

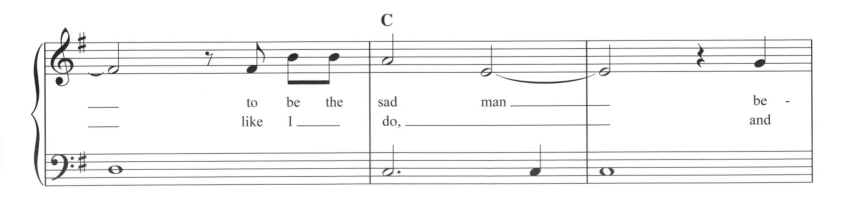

to be the sad man be -
like I do, and

hind blue eyes. _____ _____   No one knows what it's
I blame you. _____ _____   No one bites back as

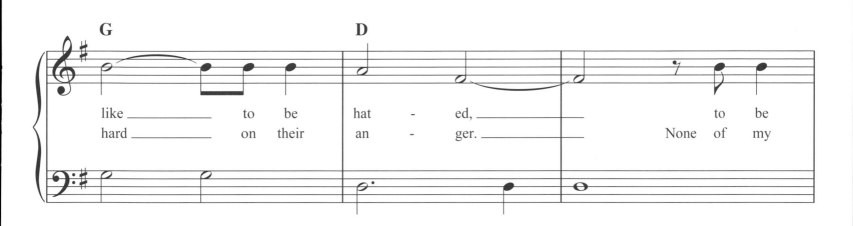

like _____ to be   hat - ed, _____   to be
hard _____ on their   an - ger. _____   None of my

fat - ed   to tell - ing   on - ly lies. _____
pain and woe   can show   through. _____

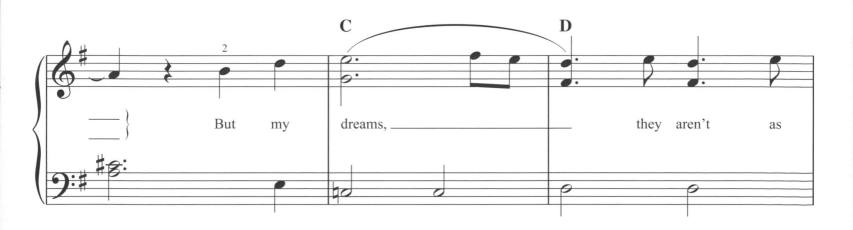

_____   But my   dreams, _____   they aren't as

empty _____ as my con - science

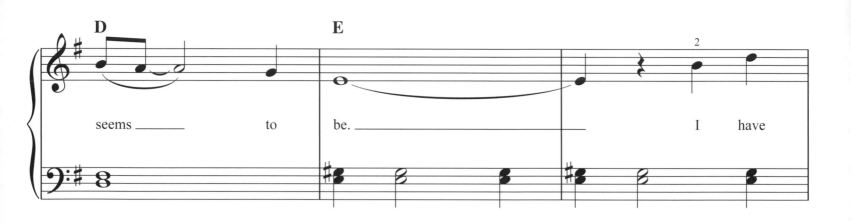

seems _____ to be. _____ I have

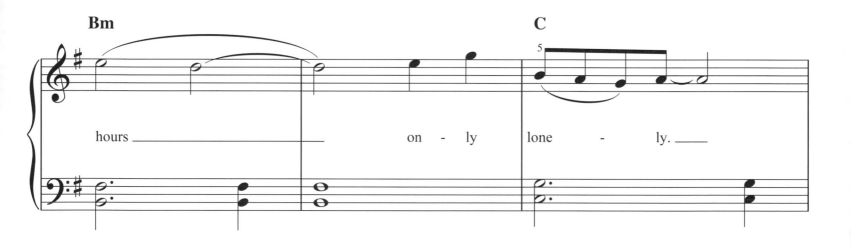

hours _____ on - ly lone - ly. ___

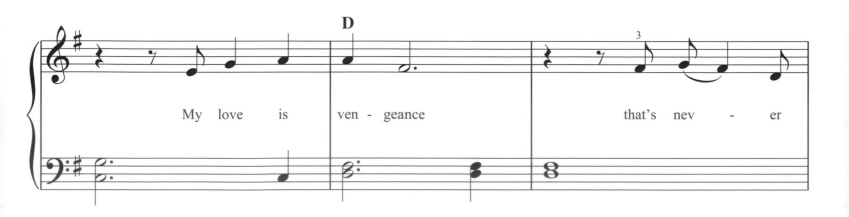

My love is ven - geance that's nev - er

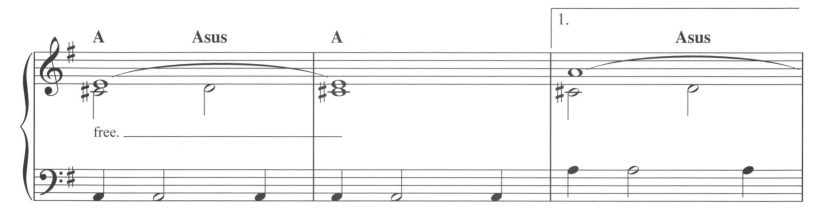

free.

When my fist

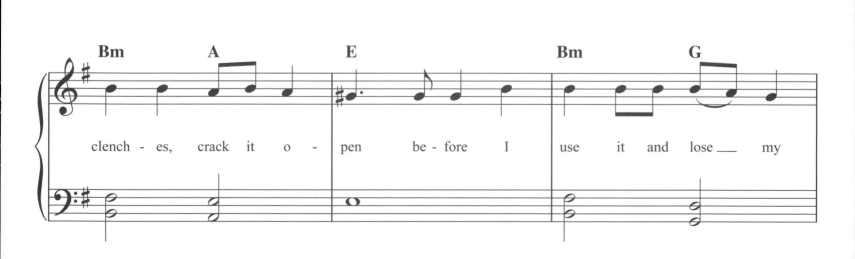

clench - es, crack it o - pen be - fore I use it and lose ___ my

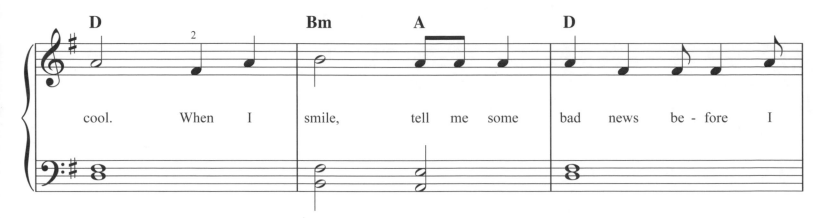

cool. When I   smile,   tell me some   bad news be - fore I

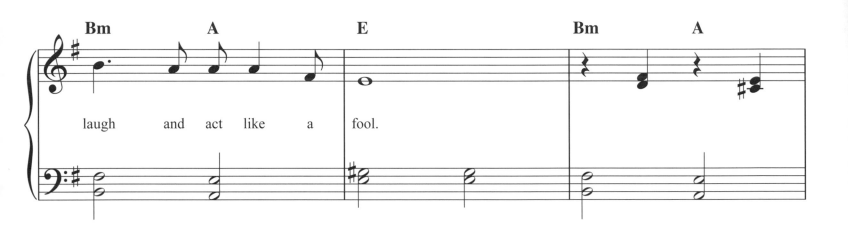

laugh   and act like a   fool.

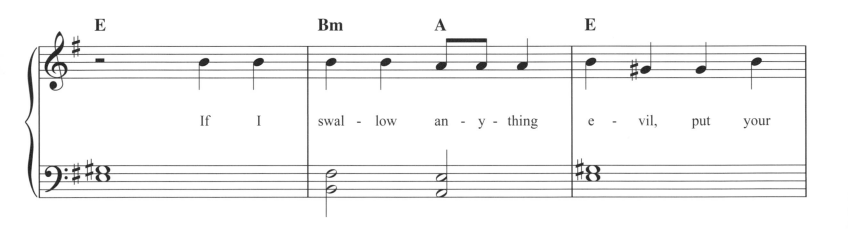

If I   swal - low an - y - thing   e - vil, put your

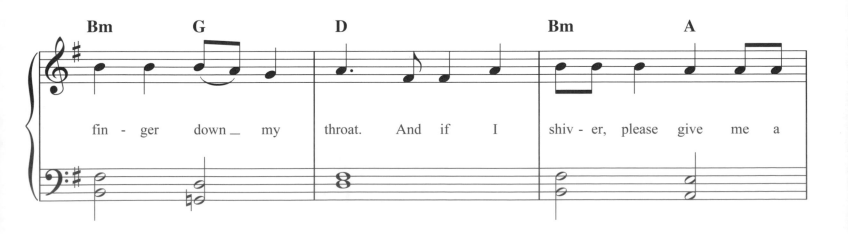

fin - ger down __ my   throat. And if I   shiv - er, please give me a

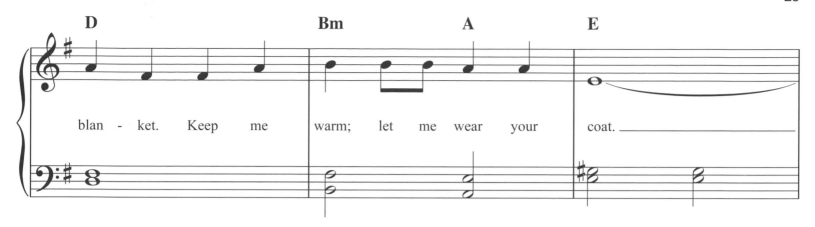

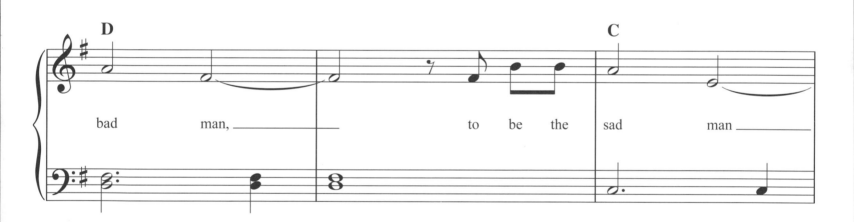

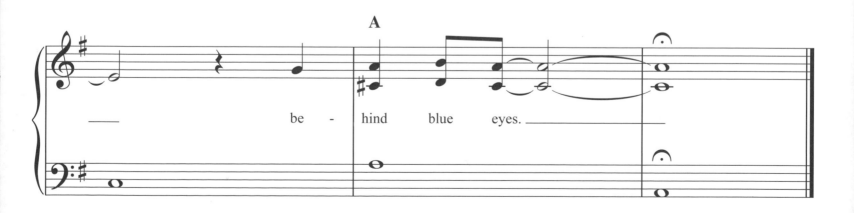

BETH

Words and Music by BOB EZRIN,
STANLEY PENRIDGE and PETER CRISS

Rock Ballad, with feeling

Beth, I hear __ you call-in', but I can't come home right now. __
You say you feel __ so emp-ty, that our house just ain't a home. __

Me and the boys __ are play-in' and we just can't find the sound. __
I'm al-ways some-where else __ and __ you're al-ways there a-lone. __

Just a few more hours, ____ and I'll be right home to you. __ I

D7   F   Am   G

think I hear them call - in'. ___ Oh, Beth, what can ___ I do?

1.
F   F/G   C   G7/C

Beth, what can ___ I do? ___

2.
F   F/G

Beth, what can ___ I do? ___

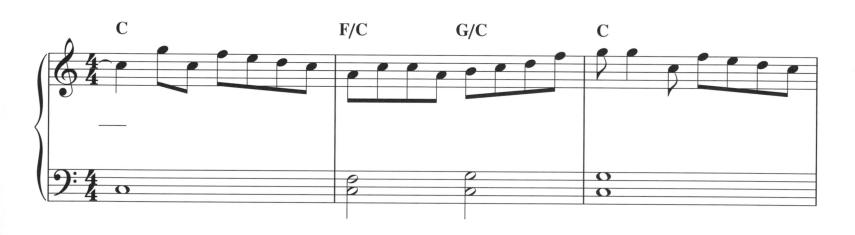

C   F/C   G/C   C

F/C   Esus E Am   G   F   E

Beth, I know __ you're lone - ly,   and I   hope you'll be   all right, __   'cause

me and the boys __ will be play - in'   all   night.

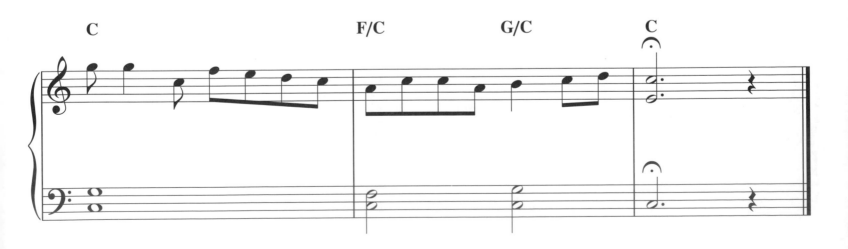

COME SAIL AWAY

Words and Music by
DENNIS DeYOUNG

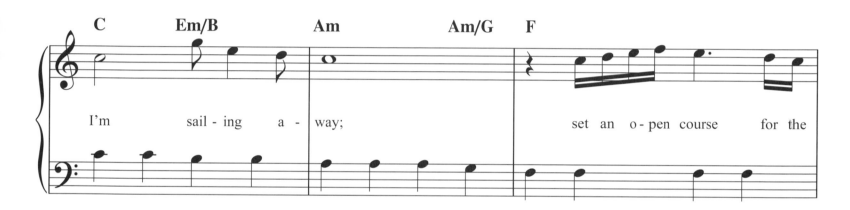

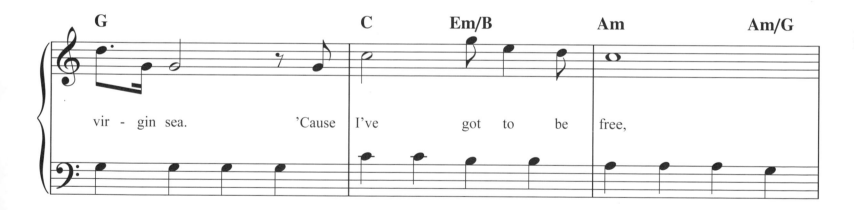

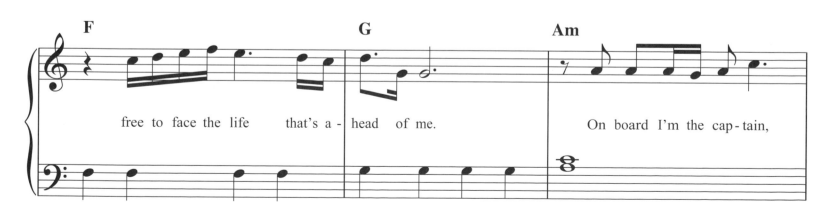

so climb a- board. We'll search for to- mor- row, on ev- 'ry shore. __ And I'll

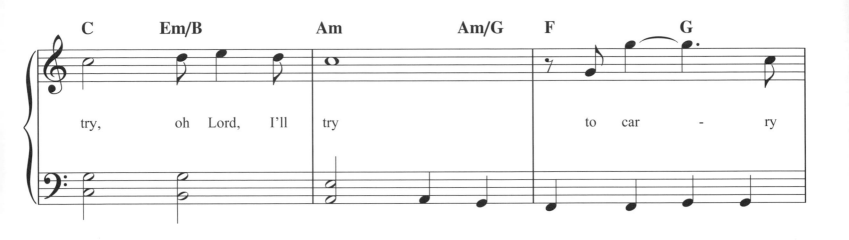

try, oh Lord, I'll try to car - ry

on.

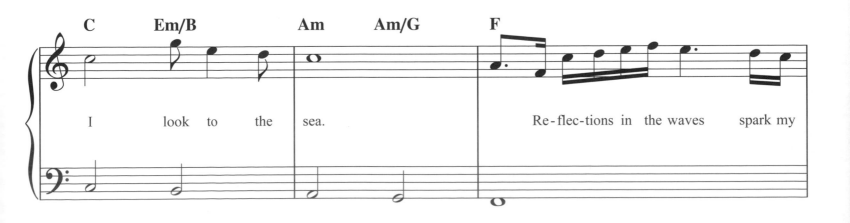

I look to the sea. Re- flec-tions in the waves spark my

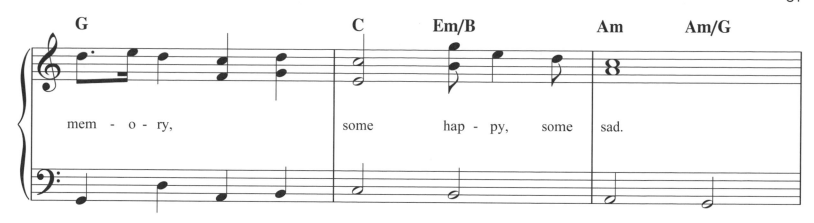

G **C** **Em/B** **Am** **Am/G**

mem - o - ry, some hap - py, some sad.

F **G** **Am**

I think of child - hood friends and the dreams we had. We lived hap - p'ly for - ev - er,

G **Am** **G**

so the sto - ry goes. But some - how we missed out on the pot of gold. ___ But we'll

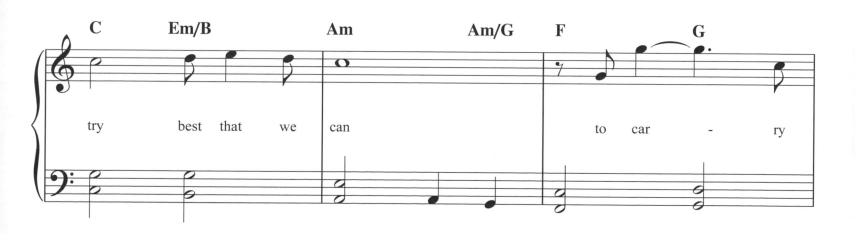

C **Em/B** **Am** **Am/G** **F** **G**

try best that we can to car - ry

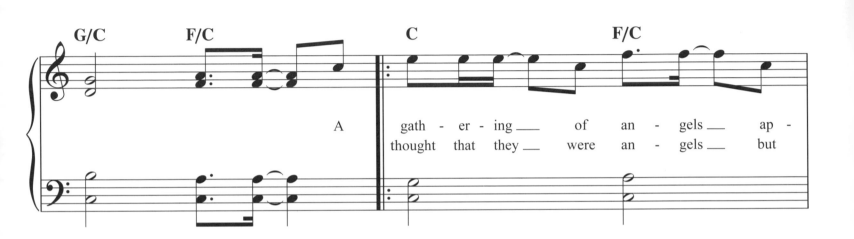

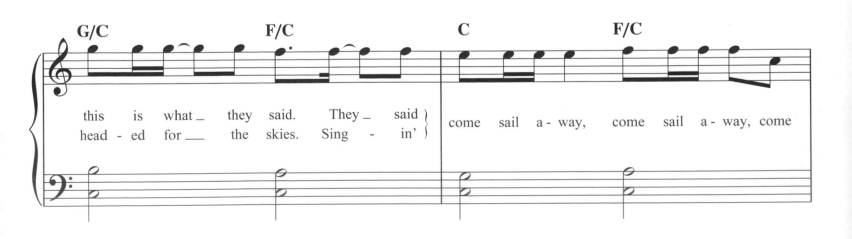

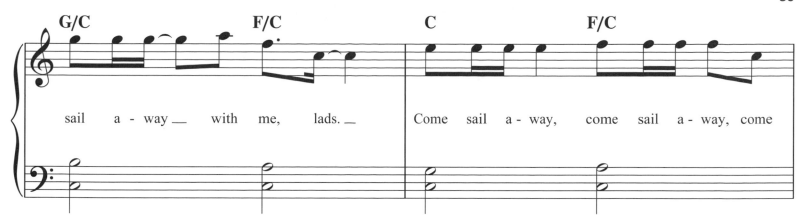

sail a - way __ with me, lads. __ Come sail a - way, come sail a - way, come

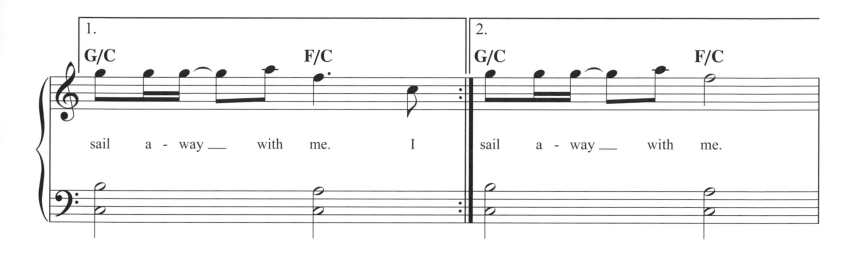

1. sail a - way __ with me. I

2. sail a - way __ with me.

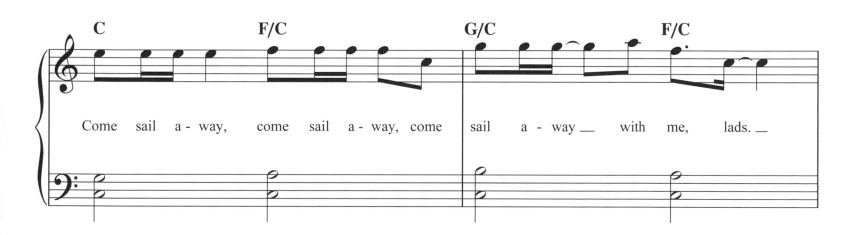

Come sail a - way, come sail a - way, come sail a - way __ with me, lads. __

Come sail a - way, come sail a - way, come sail a - way __ with me.

COLD AS ICE

Words and Music by MICK JONES
and LOU GRAMM

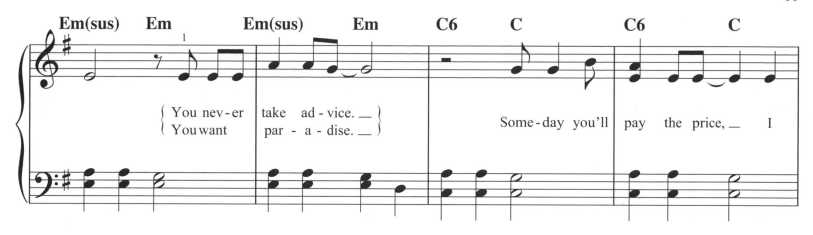

Em(sus) Em Em(sus) Em C6 C C6 C

{ You nev-er take ad-vice. __ }
{ You want par-a-dise. __ }

Some-day you'll pay the price, __ I

Am G F#+

know. I've seen it be-fore; __ it hap-pens all the time. __ You're

Am C C/D G

clos-ing the door; __ you leave the world be-hind. __ You're dig-ging for gold __ yet

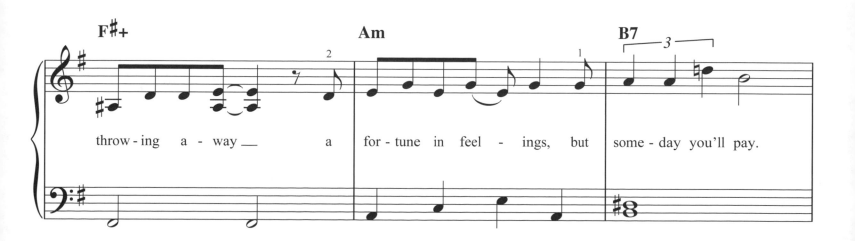

F#+ Am B7

throw-ing a-way __ a for-tune in feel-ings, but some-day you'll pay.

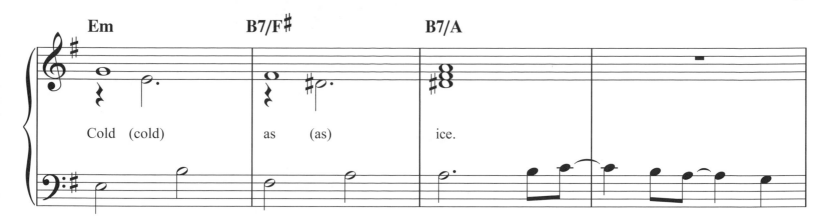

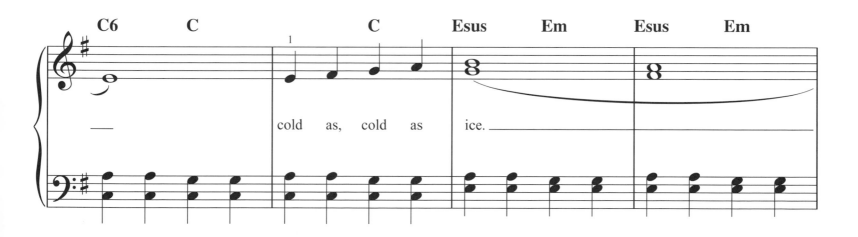

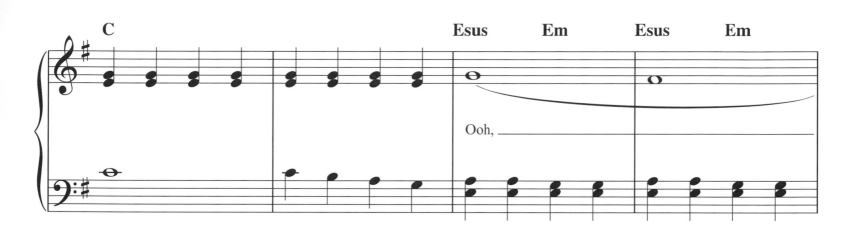

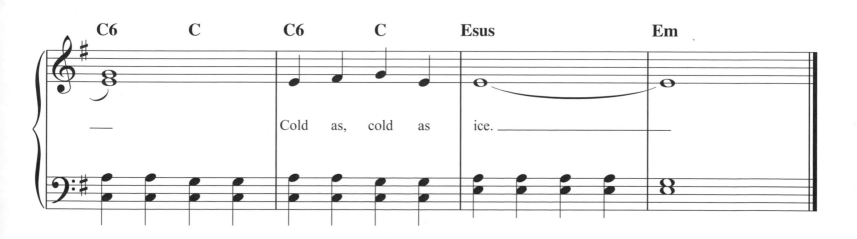

COLOUR MY WORLD

Words and Music by
JAMES PANKOW

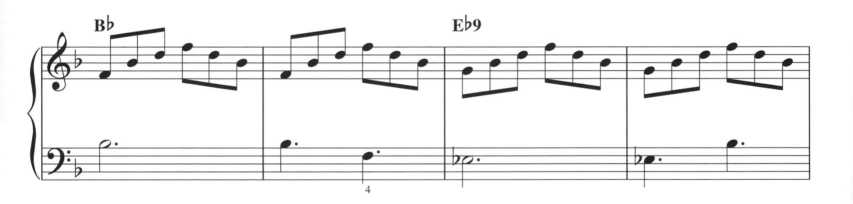

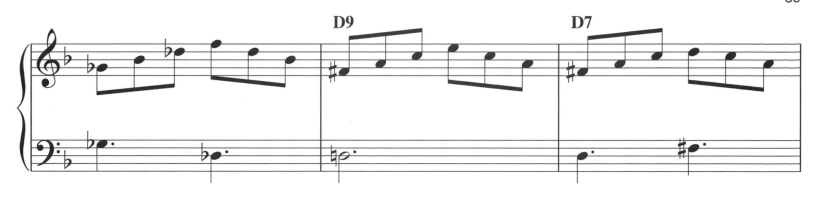

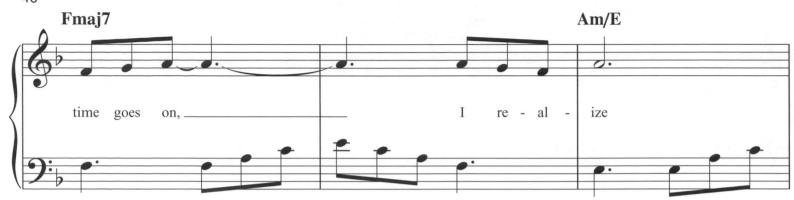

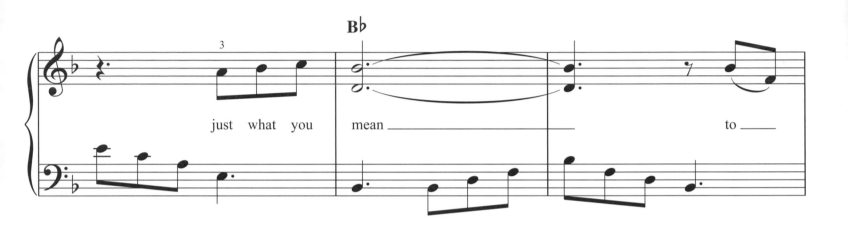

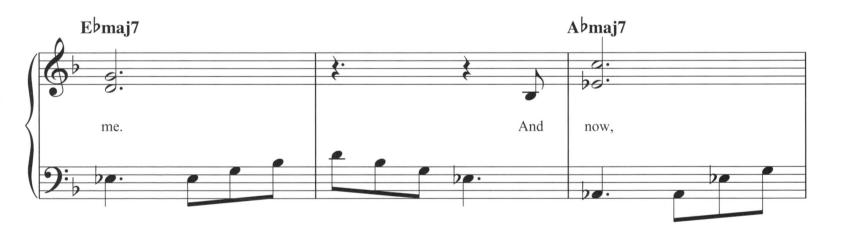

D   **D7**   **Gmaj7**

love   that I've wait - ed to   share.

Eb7

And dreams   of our mo - ments to -

C7

geth - er, _____   col - our my world _____ with

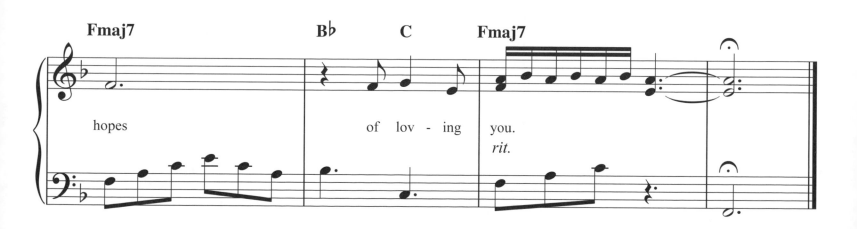

Fmaj7   **Bb**   **C**   **Fmaj7**

hopes   of lov - ing you.

rit.

DO IT AGAIN

Words and Music by WALTER BECKER
and WALTER FAGEN

catch you at the bor - der. And the mourn - ers are all sing-
sure you're near the end. Then you love a lit - tle wild
han - dle in your hand. Your black cards can make you mon-

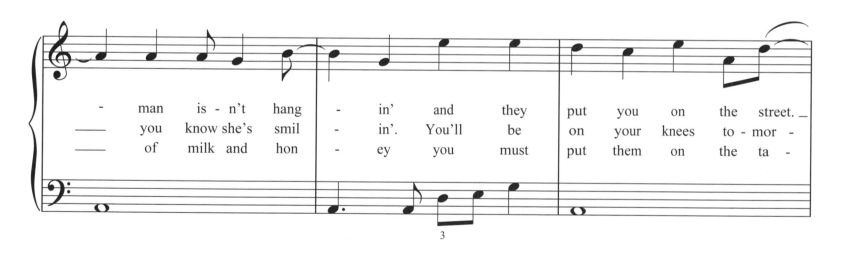

- in' as they drag you by your feet, but the hang-
one and she brings you on - ly sor - row; all the time
- ey so you hide them when you're a - ble; in the land

- man is - n't hang - in' and they put you on the street.
you know she's smil - in'. You'll be on your knees to - mor -
of milk and hon - ey you must put them on the ta -

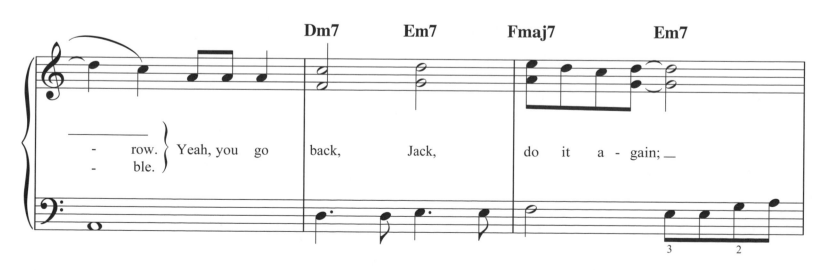

Dm7   **Em7**   **Fmaj7**   **Em7**

- row. } Yeah, you go back, Jack, do it a - gain; __
- ble.

44

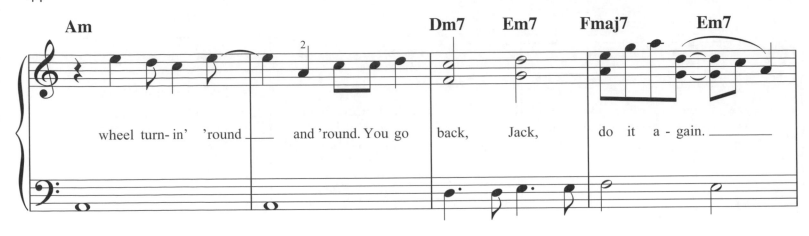

Am   Dm7   Em7   Fmaj7   Em7

wheel turn- in' 'round ____ and 'round. You go   back,   Jack,   do it a - gain. ____ ____

Am7

1., 2.

E7sus

When you   know __
Now you   swear __

3.

E7sus   Am7

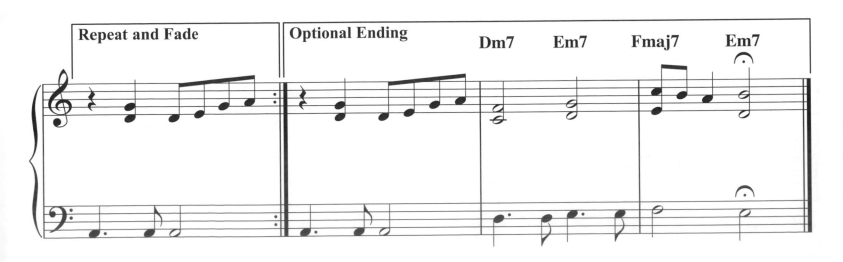

Repeat and Fade   **Optional Ending**   Dm7   Em7   Fmaj7   Em7

DON'T DREAM IT'S OVER

Words and Music by
NEIL FINN

There is   free - dom with - in;
Now I'm   tow - ing my   car;
Now I'm   walk - ing a - gain

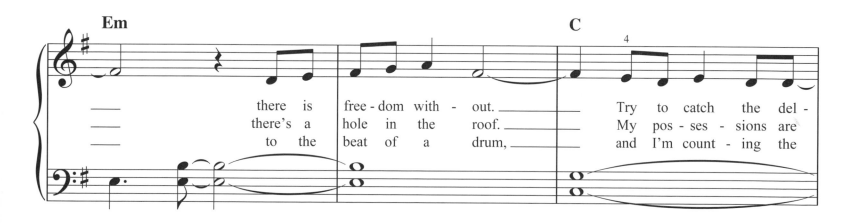

there is   free - dom with - out.   Try to catch the del -
there's a   hole in the   roof.   My pos - ses - sions are
to the   beat of a   drum,   and I'm count - ing the

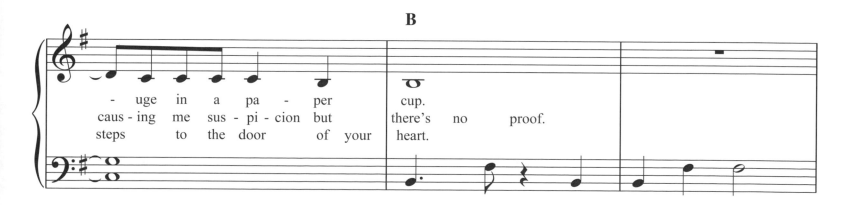

- uge in a pa - per   cup.
caus - ing me sus - pi - cion but   there's no   proof.
steps   to   the   door   of your   heart.

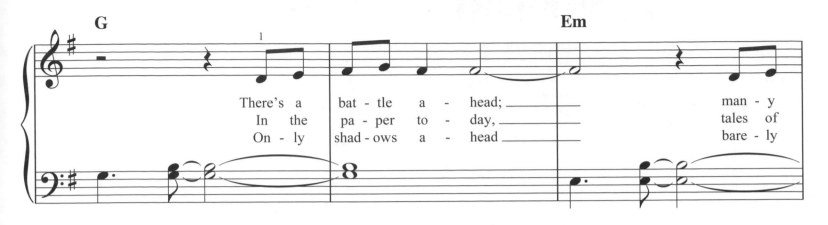

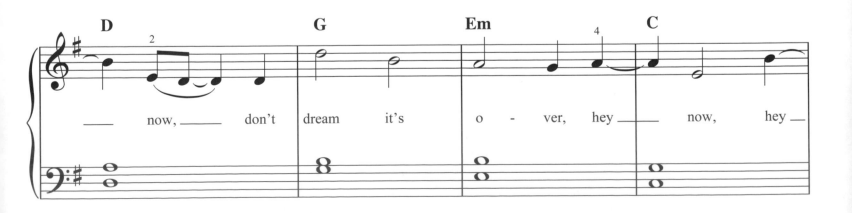

47

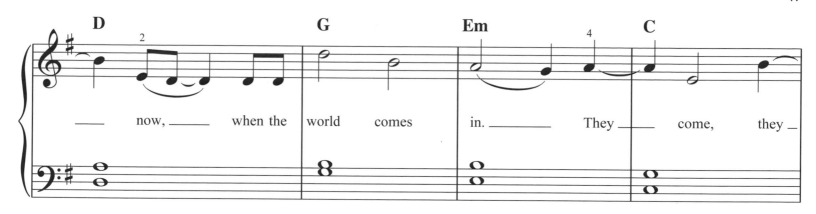

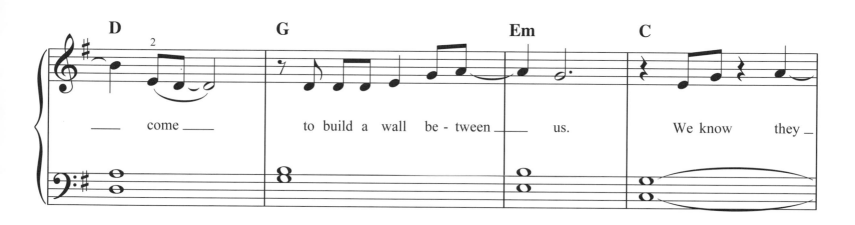

now, _____ when the world comes in. _____ They _____ come, they _____

come _____ to build a wall be-tween _____ us. We know they _____

_____ won't _ win. _____

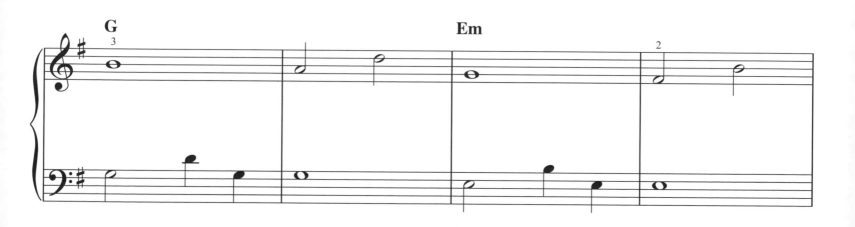

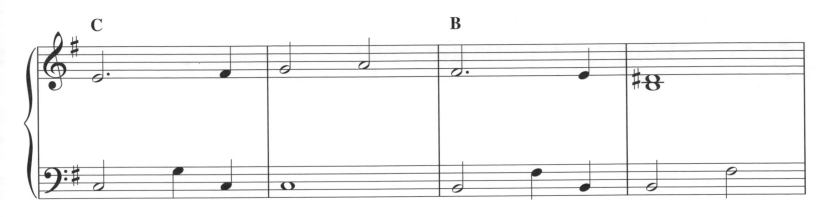

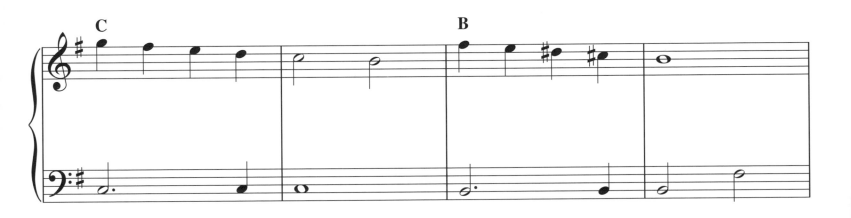

D.S. al Coda

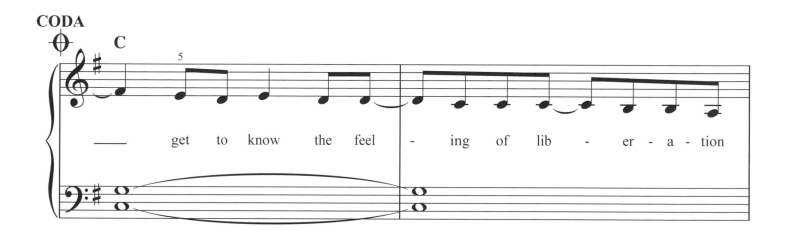

CODA

get to know the feel - ing of lib - er - a - tion

and re - lease. _____ Hey _____ now, _____ hey _____

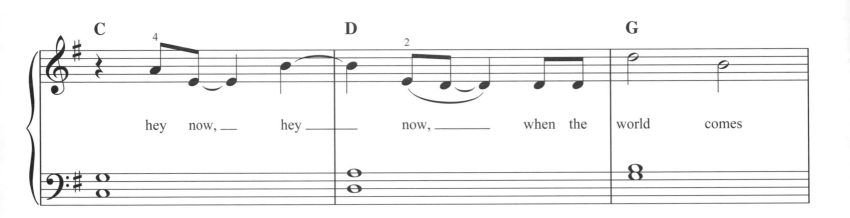

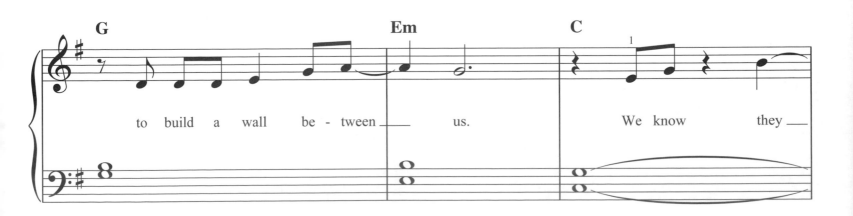

won't __ win. _____

D **G** **Em**

Don't let them win. __

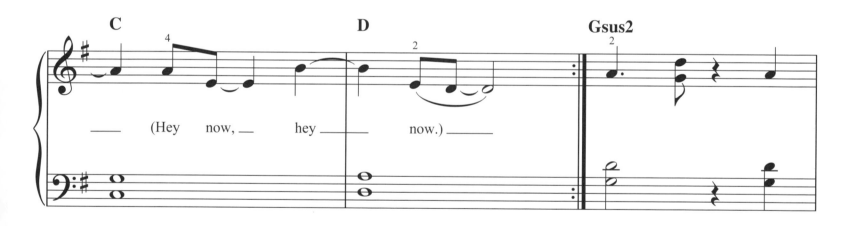

C **D** **Gsus2**

__ (Hey now, __ hey _____ now.) _____

EVIL WOMAN

Words and Music by
JEFF LYNNE

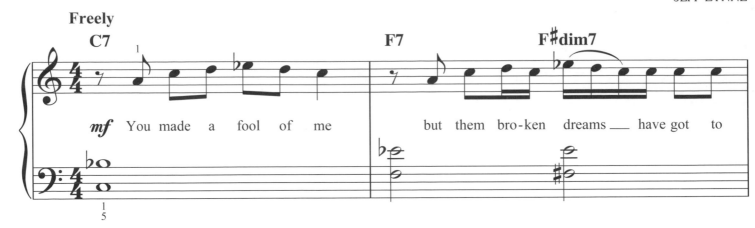

You made a fool of me but them bro-ken dreams ___ have got to

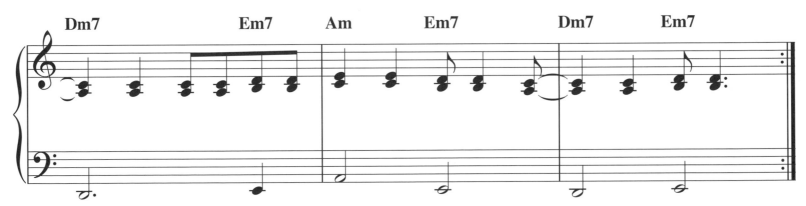

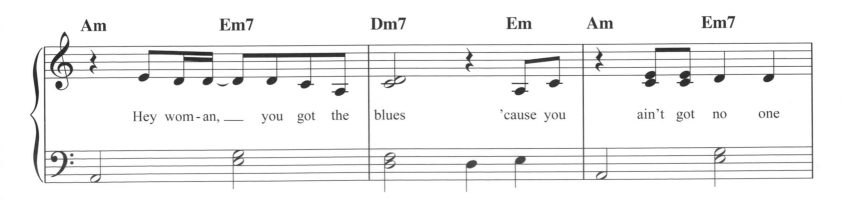

Hey wom-an, ___ you got the blues 'cause you ain't got no one

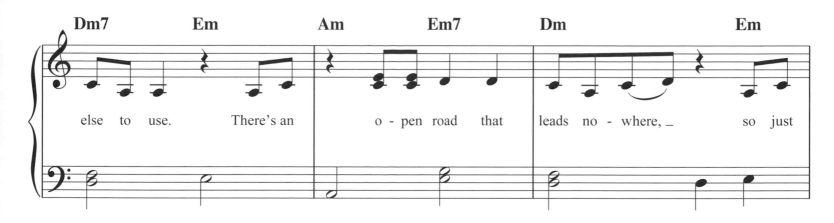

else to use.   There's an   o - pen road that   leads no - where, __   so just

make some miles be - tween here   and there.   There's a   hole in my head __ where the

rain comes in,   you took my bod - y and   played to win.

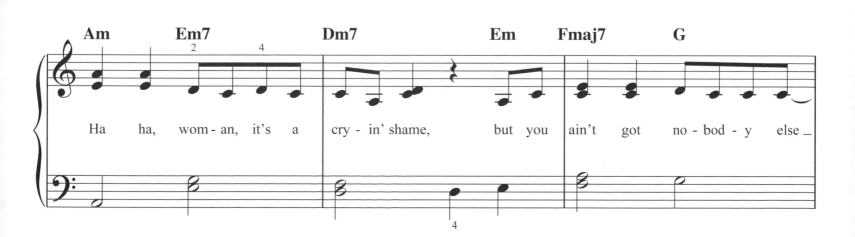

Ha   ha, wom - an, it's a   cry - in' shame,   but you   ain't got   no - bod - y   else __

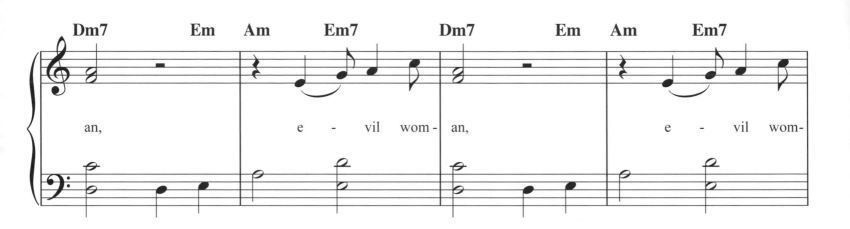

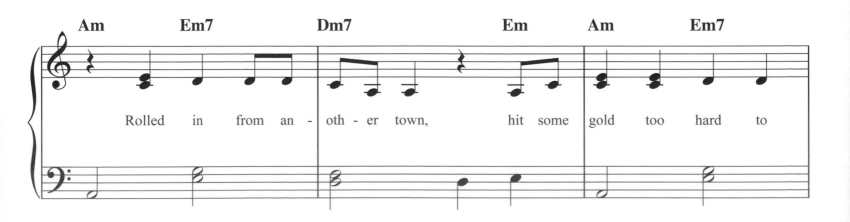

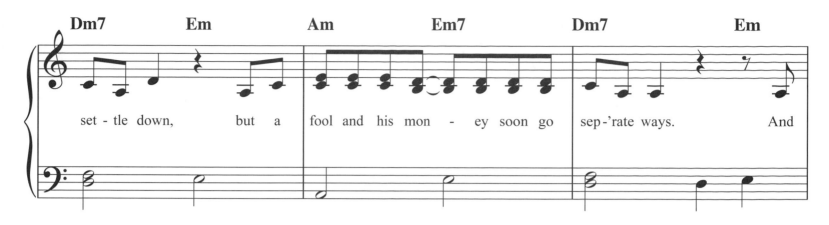

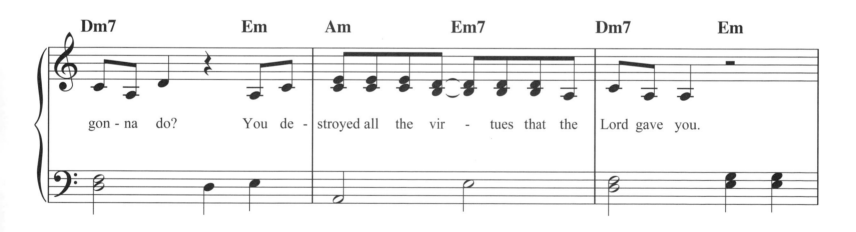

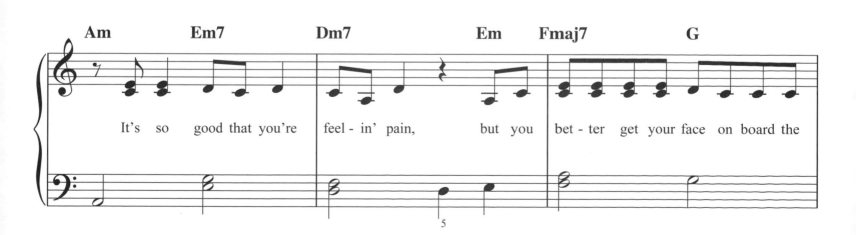

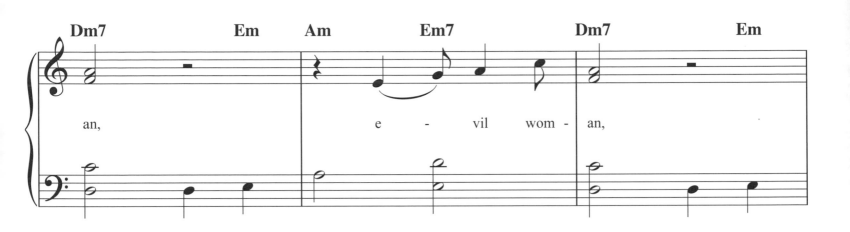

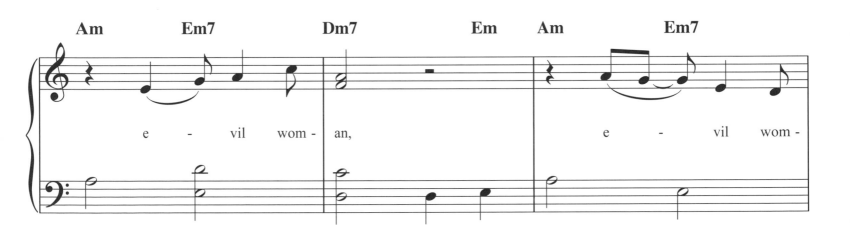

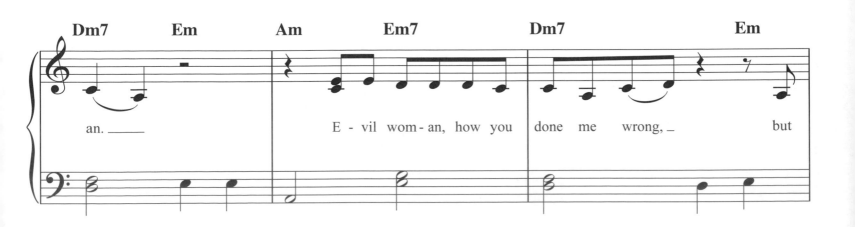

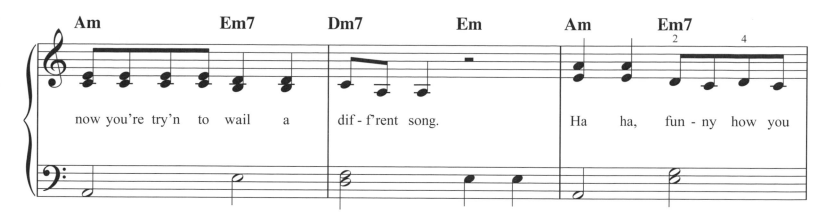

now you're try'n to wail a dif-f'rent song. Ha ha, fun-ny how you

broke me up; you made the wine, now you drink a cup.

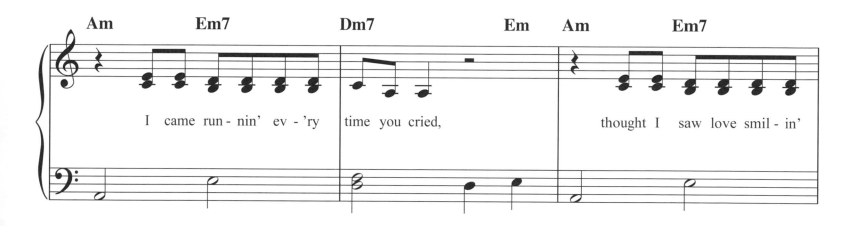

I came run-nin' ev-'ry time you cried, thought I saw love smil-in'

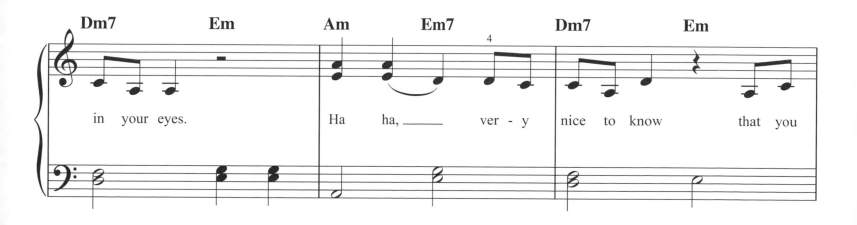

in your eyes. Ha ha, _____ ver-y nice to know that you

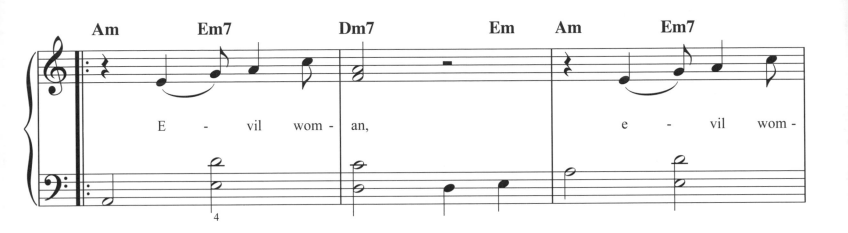

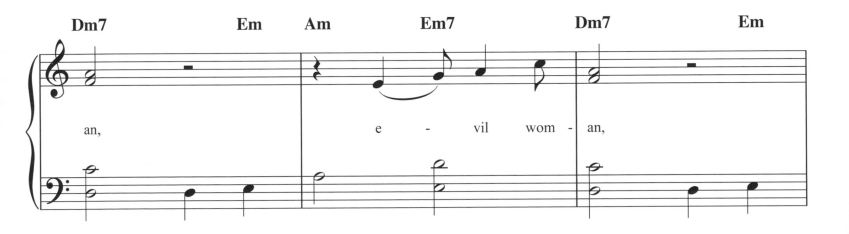

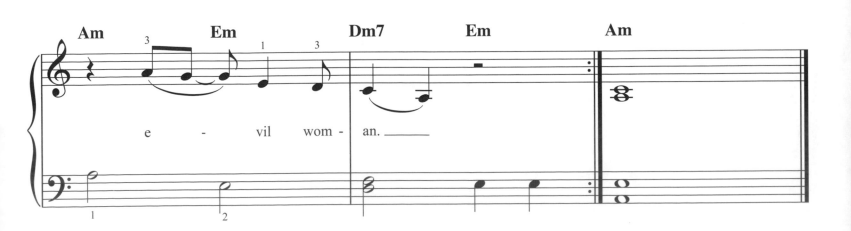

DREAM ON

Words and Music by
STEVEN TYLER

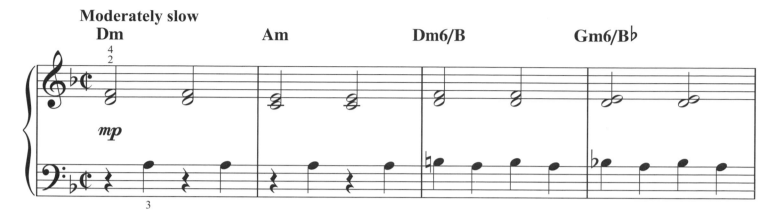

Ev - 'ry time_____ that I look in the mir - ror,

all these lines on my face get- tin' clear - er.

The past___ is gone;_____

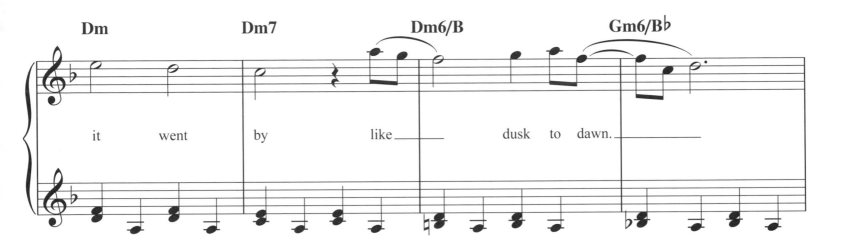

it went by like___ dusk to dawn.___

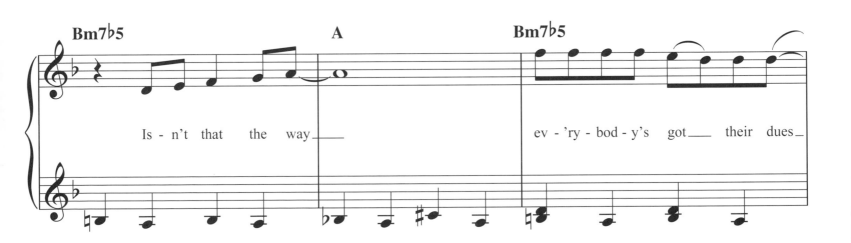

Is - n't that the way___ ev - 'ry - bod - y's got___ their dues___

_____ in life___ to pay?___

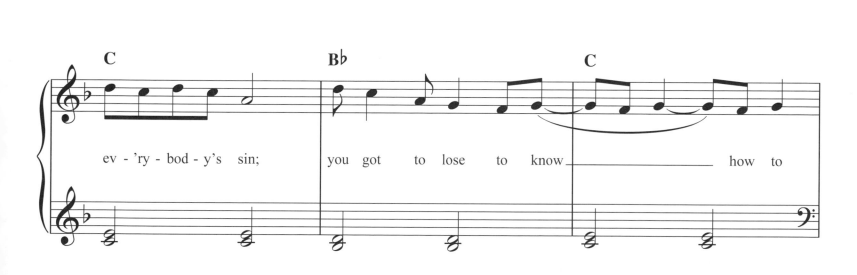

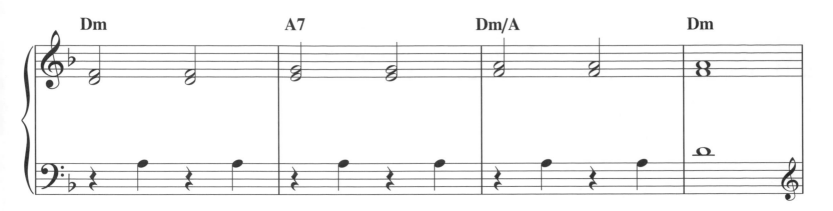

Half my life's in books' writ-ten pag - es,

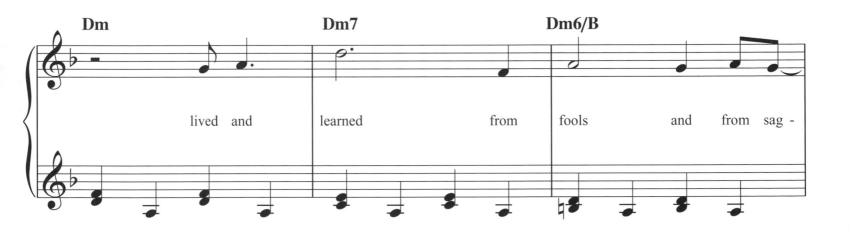

lived and learned from fools and from sag -

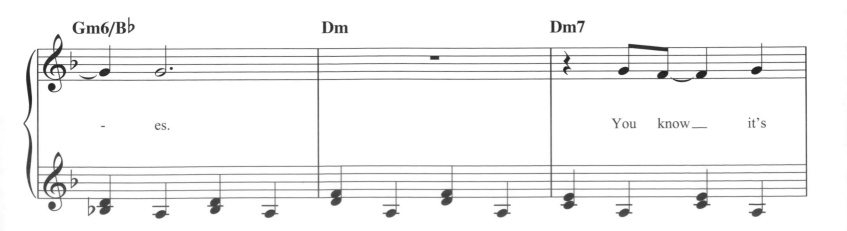

- es. You know___ it's

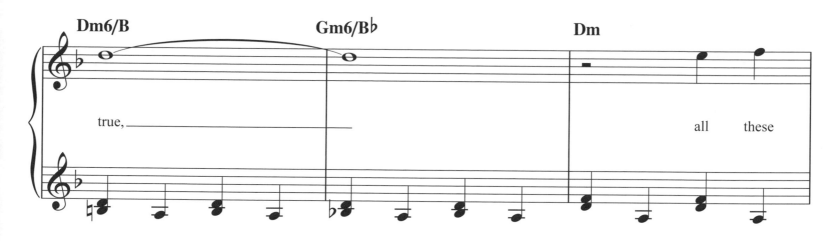

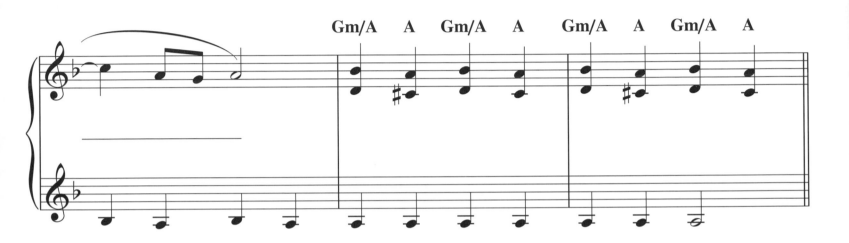

1.

Bb ... C

maybe to-mor-row the good Lord will take you a - way.

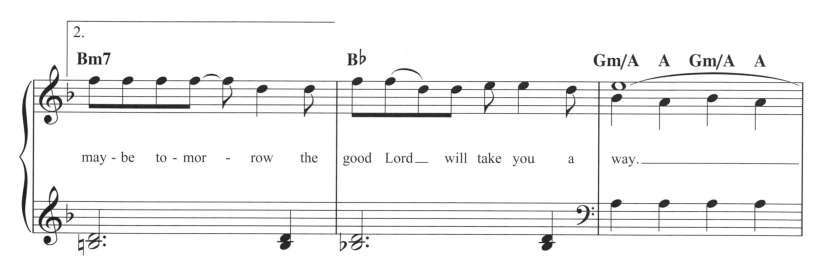

2.

Bm7 ... Bb ... Gm/A A Gm/A A

maybe to-mor-row the good Lord will take you a way.

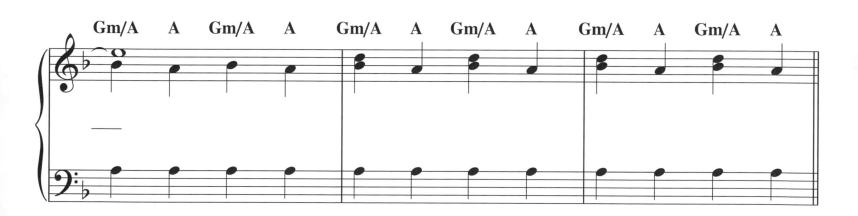

Gm/A A Gm/A A Gm/A A Gm/A A Gm/A A Gm/A A

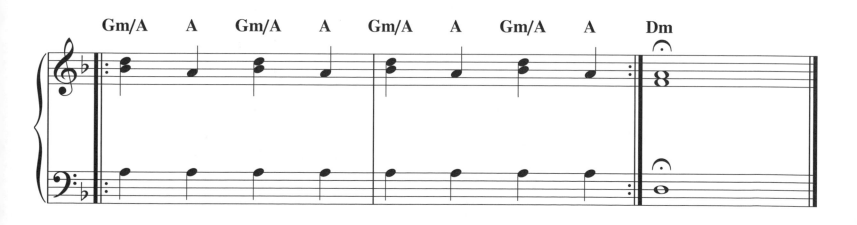

Gm/A A Gm/A A Gm/A A Gm/A A Dm

THE END OF THE INNOCENCE

Words and Music by BRUCE HORNSBY
and DON HENLEY

Moderately fast

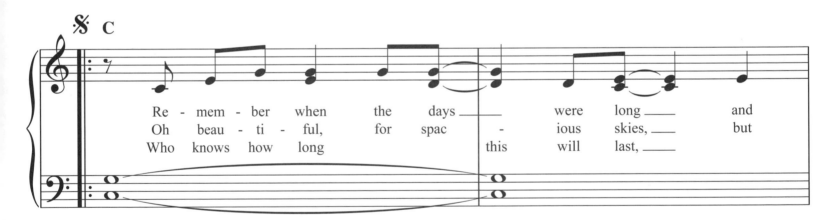

Re - mem - ber when the days ____ were long ____ and
Oh beau - ti - ful, for spac ____ - ious skies, ____ but
Who knows how long this will last, ____

rolled be - neath ____ a deep blue sky? ____
now those skies ____ are threat - en - ing. ____
now we've come ____ so far so fast? ____

67

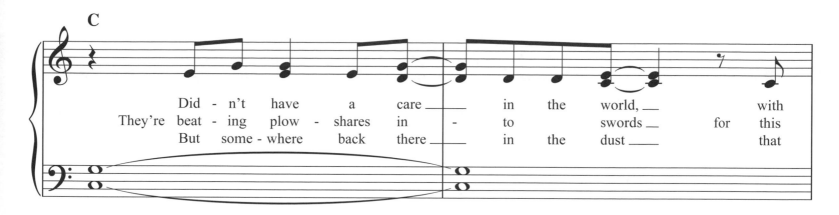

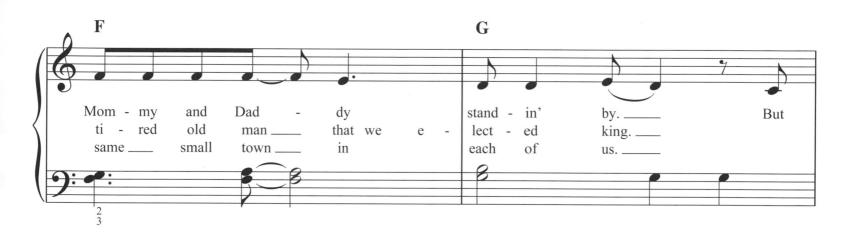

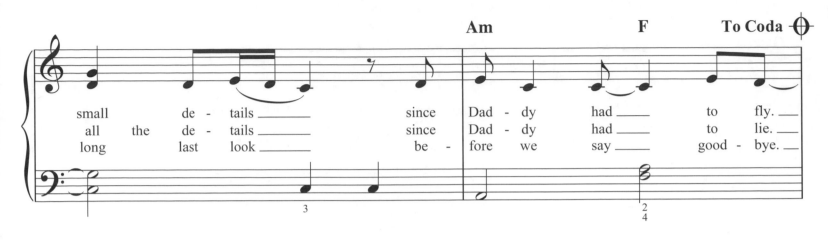

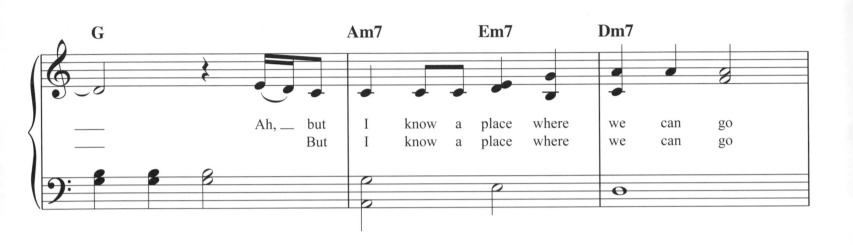

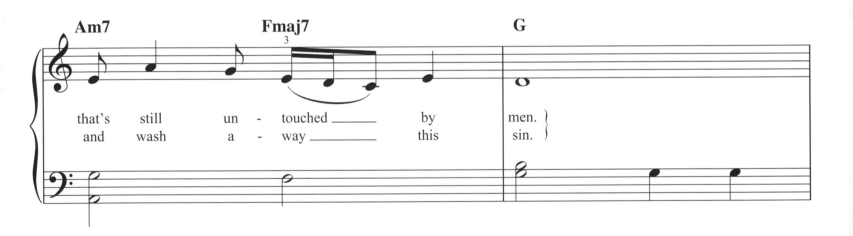

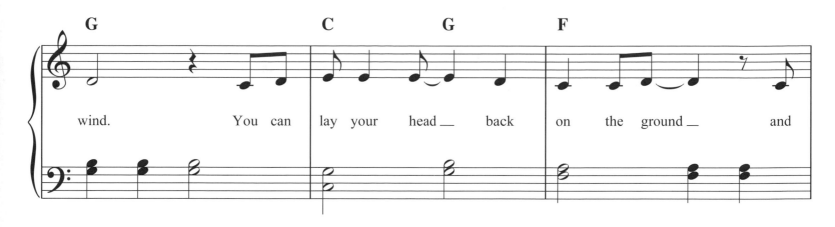

wind.   You can   lay   your   head __   back   on   the   ground __   and

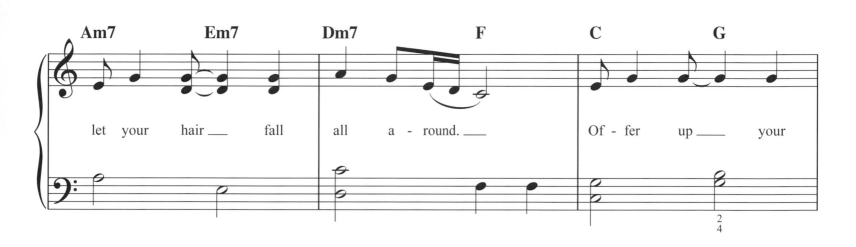

let   your   hair __   fall   all   a - round. __   Of - fer   up __   your

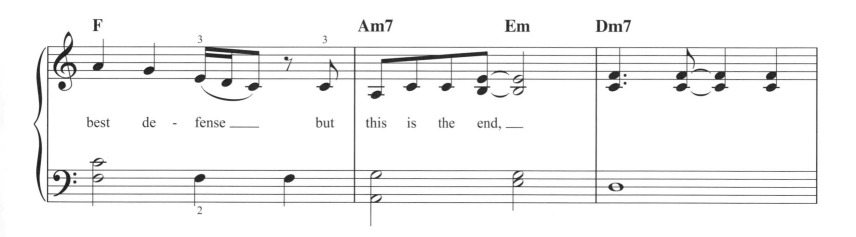

best   de - fense __   but   this   is   the   end, __

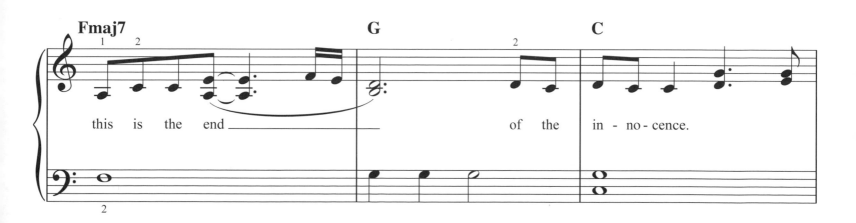

this   is   the   end _____   of   the   in - no - cence.

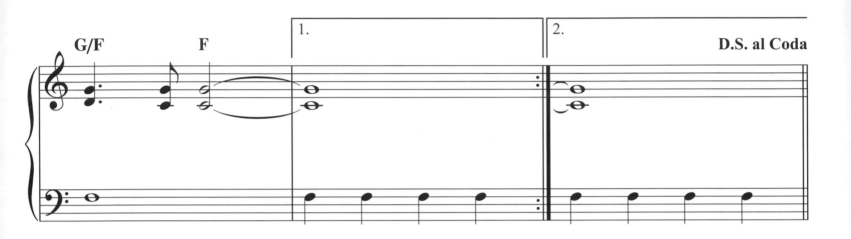

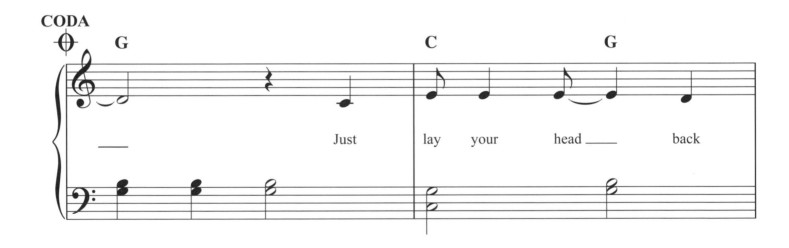

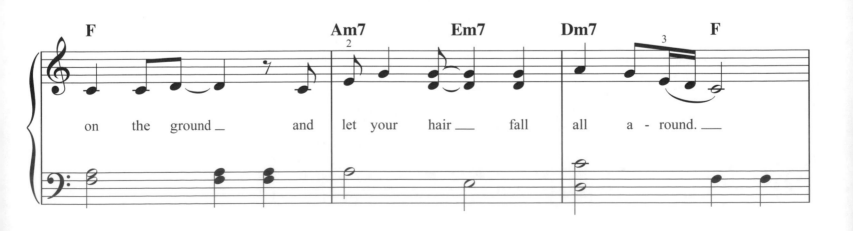

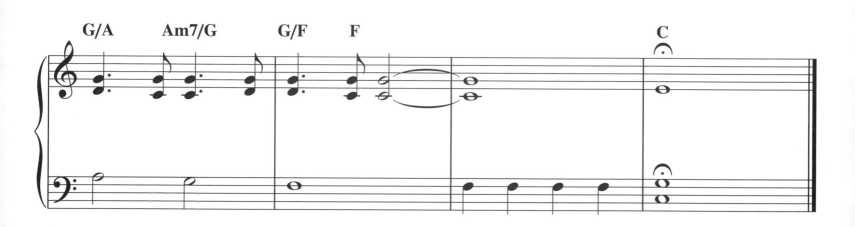

(Everything I Do)
I DO IT FOR YOU

from the Motion Picture ROBIN HOOD: PRINCE OF THIEVES

Words and Music by BRYAN ADAMS,
R.J. LANGE and MICHAEL KAMEN

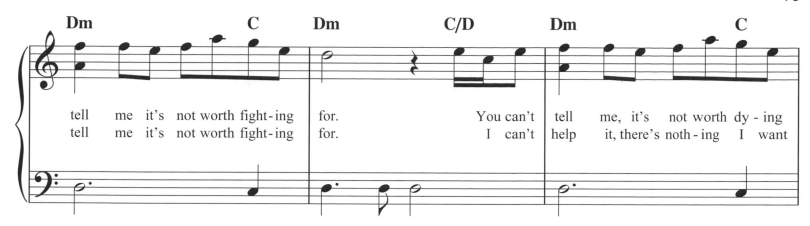

tell   me   it's not worth fight-ing   for.   You can't   tell   me, it's   not worth dy - ing

tell   me   it's not worth fight-ing   for.   I   can't   help   it, there's noth - ing I   want

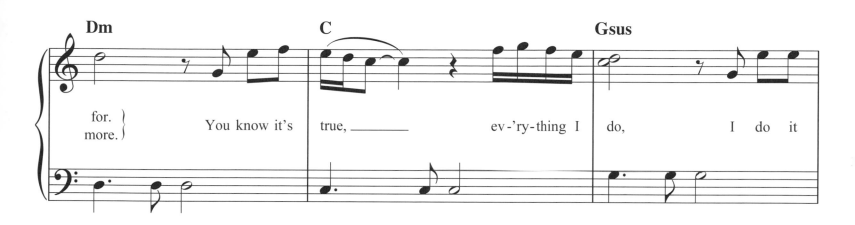

for.

more.   You know it's   true, _____   ev-'ry-thing I   do,   I   do it

1.   2.

for you. _____   for you. _____   There's

no love   like   your love, _____   and no   oth - er   could give

more _____ love.   There's   no ____ way, _____   un - less   you're ____ there   all   the

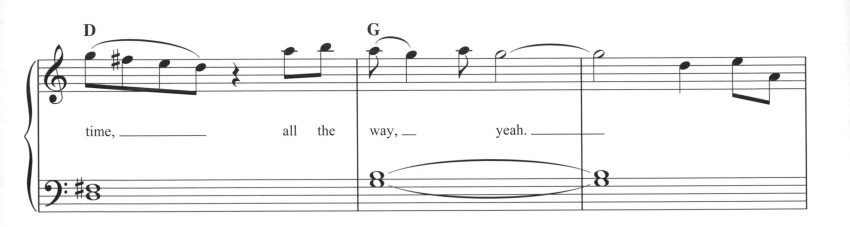

time, _____   all   the   way, ____   yeah. _____

Oh, you can't

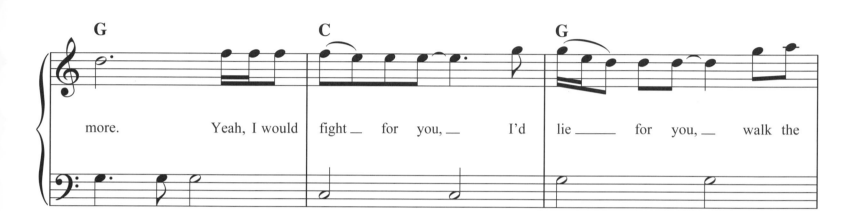

FREE BIRD

Words and Music by ALLEN COLLINS
and RONNIE VAN ZANT

If I leave here to - mor - row,
Bye, bye ba - by, it's been a | sweet love,

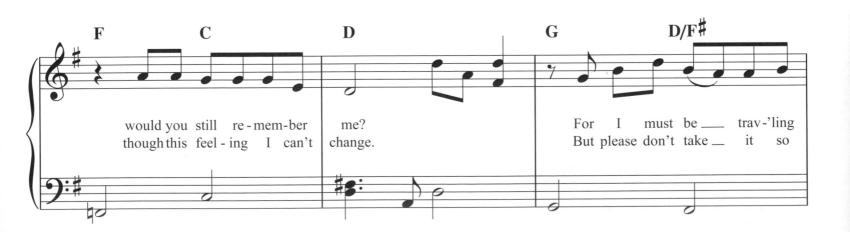

would you still re - mem - ber | me?
though this feel - ing I can't | change.

For I must be ___ trav - 'ling
But please don't take ___ it so

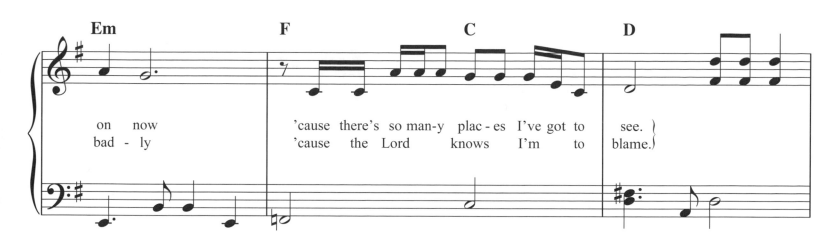

on now 'cause there's so man-y plac-es I've got to see.
bad - ly 'cause the Lord knows I'm to blame.

But if I stayed here with you, girl, things just could-n't be the

same. 'Cause I'm as free as a bird now.

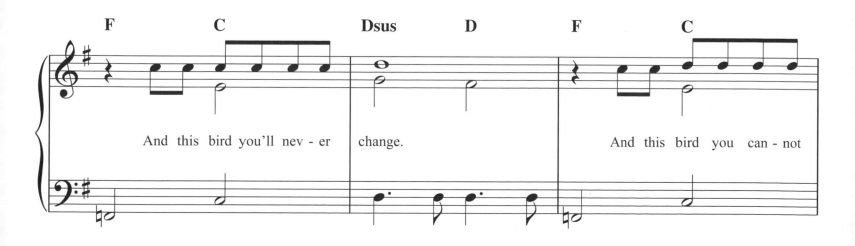

And this bird you'll nev - er change. And this bird you can - not

GIMME SOME LOVIN'

Words and Music by STEVE WINWOOD,
MUFF WINWOOD and SPENCER DAVIS

Let me in, ba - by, I don't know what you've got, but you'd bet- ter take it eas - y. This
Been a hard day __ and I don't know what to do. Wait a min- ute, ba - by. It could
Been a hard day, __ noth- in' went too good. Now I'm gon - na re - lax, hon - ey. Ev - 'ry -

__ place is hot.
hap - pen to you.
bod - y should.

So glad __ we made __ it,

so glad __ we made __ it.

Gim-me some lov - in',

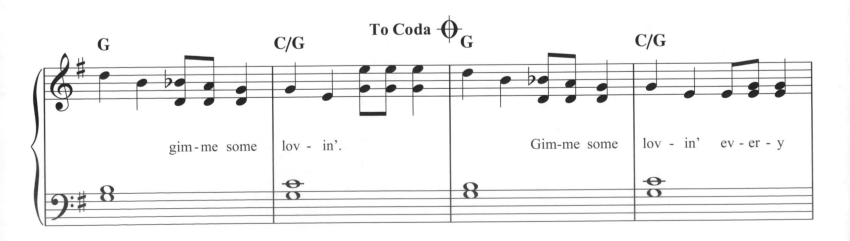

gim-me some lov - in'.

Gim-me some lov - in' ev - er - y

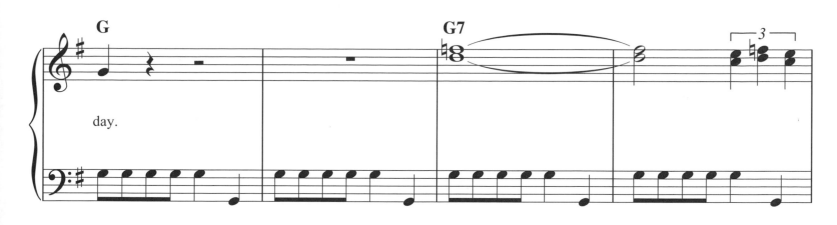

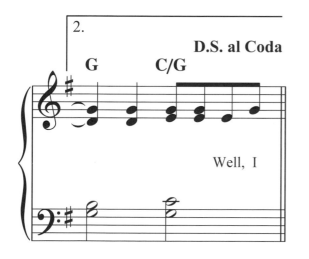

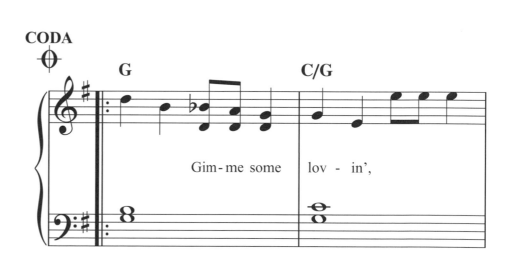

FREE FALLIN'

Words and Music by TOM PETTY
and JEFF LYNNE

It's a long day ___
vam - pires ___
glide down ___

liv - in' in Re - se - da. There's a free - way ___
walk - in' through the val - ley ___ move west down ___
o - ver Mul - hol - land. ___ I wan - na write her ___

run - nin' through the yard. ___ And I'm a bad boy ___ 'cause I
Ven - tur - a Boul - e - vard. And all the bad boys ___ are
name _ in the sky. ___ I wan - na free fall ___

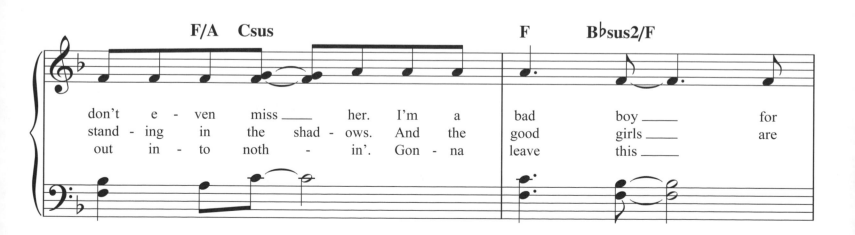

don't e - ven miss ___ her. I'm a bad boy ___ for
stand - ing in the shad - ows. And the good girls ___ are
out in - to noth - in'. Gon - na leave this ___

break-in' her heart. ___
home with bro-ken hearts. }
world for a while. ___
And I'm free, free

fall - in'. Yeah, I'm free,

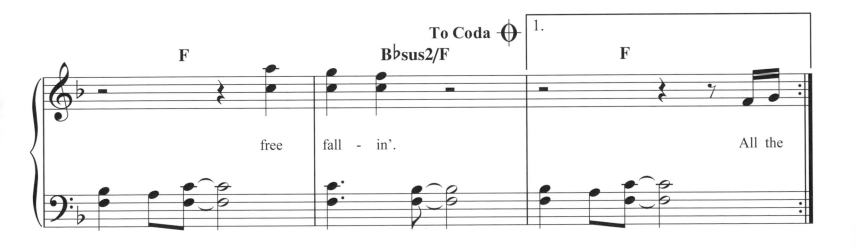

To Coda

free fall - in'. All the

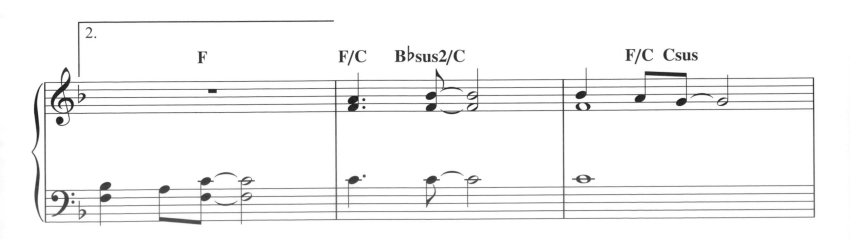

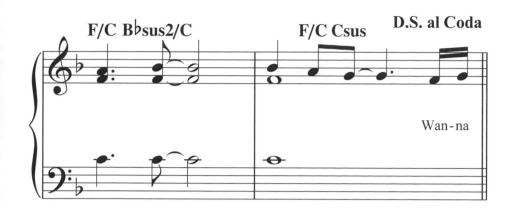

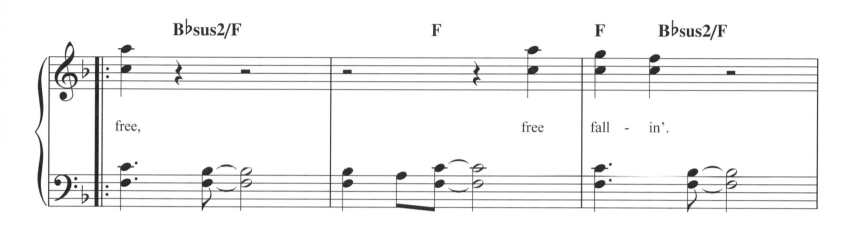

HAVE I TOLD YOU LATELY

Words and Music by
VAN MORRISON

Slowly, with expression

Have I told you late-ly that I love you? _____ Have I

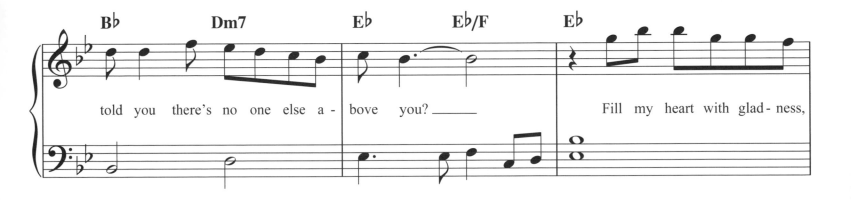

told you there's no one else a-bove you? _____ Fill my heart with glad-ness,

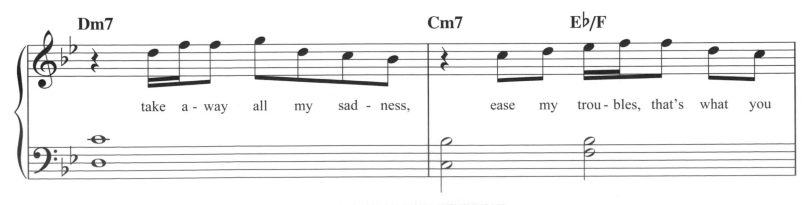

take a-way all my sad-ness, ease my trou-bles, that's what you

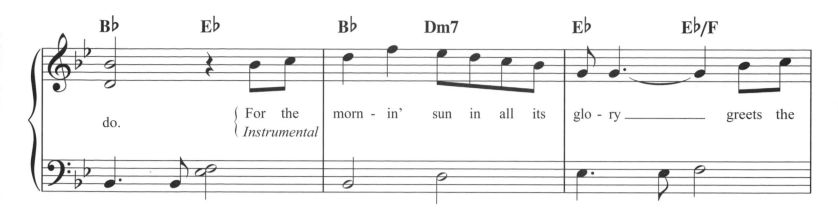

do. { For the morn - in' sun in all its glo - ry _____ greets the
    { *Instrumental*

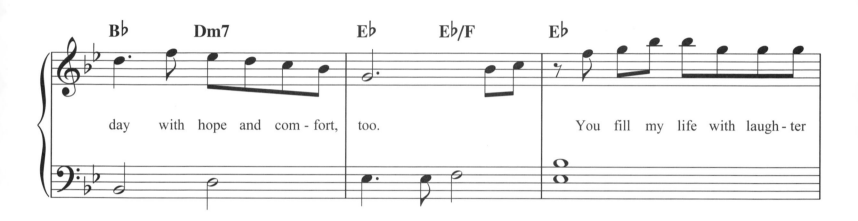

day with hope and com - fort, too. You fill my life with laugh - ter

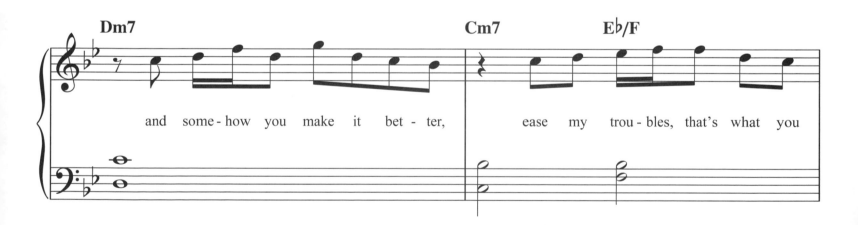

and some - how you make it bet - ter, ease my trou - bles, that's what you

do. There's a love that's di - vine and it's yours and it's mine __
Instrumental ends

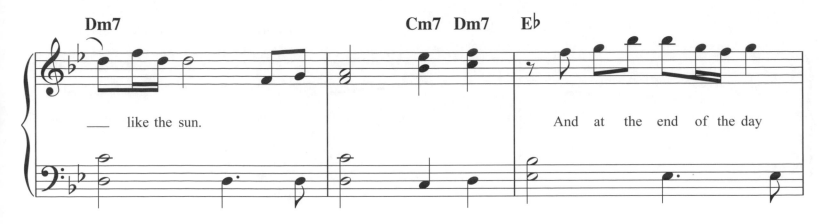

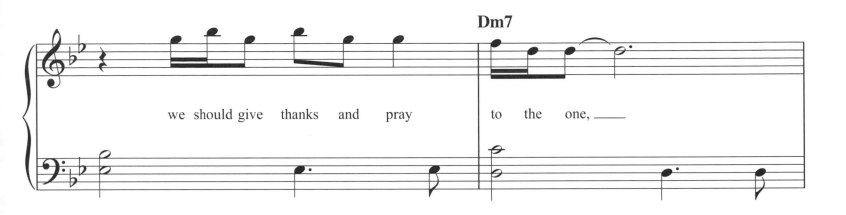

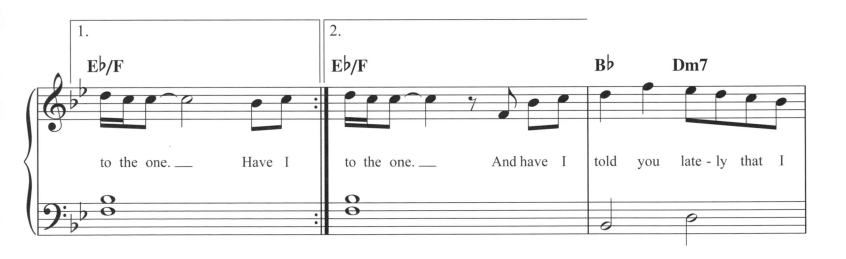

You fill my heart with glad-ness, take a-way my sad-ness, ease my trou-bles, that's what you

do. Take a-way all my sad-ness, fill my life with glad-ness,

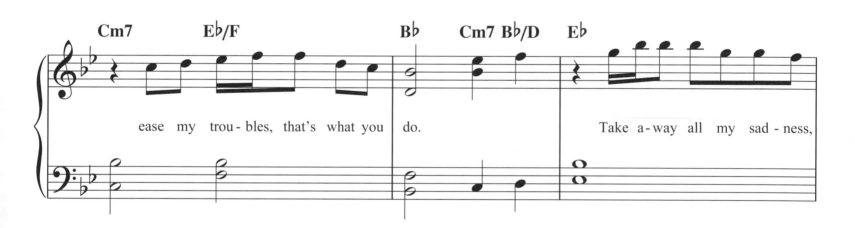

ease my trou-bles, that's what you do. Take a-way all my sad-ness,

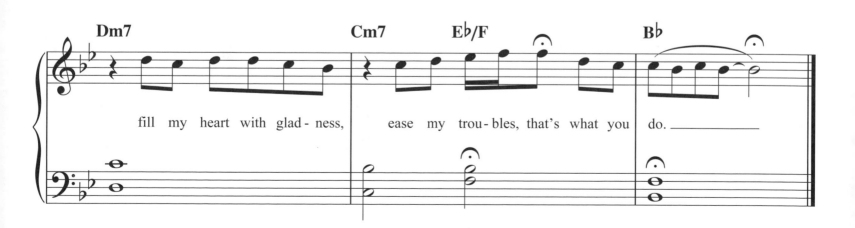

fill my heart with glad-ness, ease my trou-bles, that's what you do. _____

HELLO, IT'S ME

Words and Music by
TODD RUNDGREN

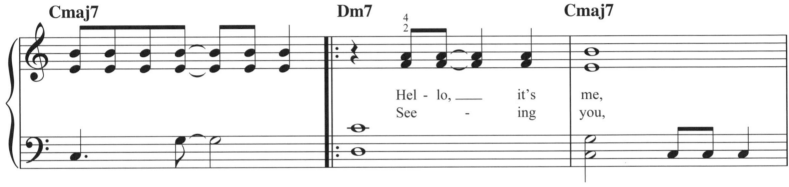

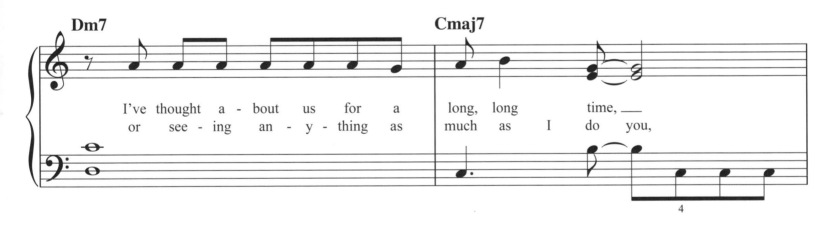

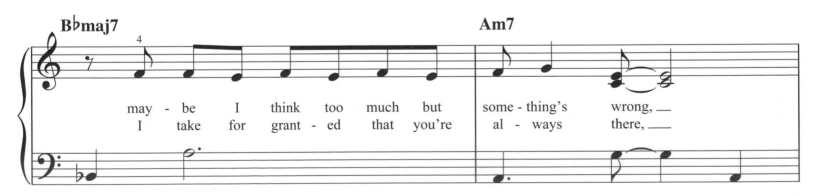

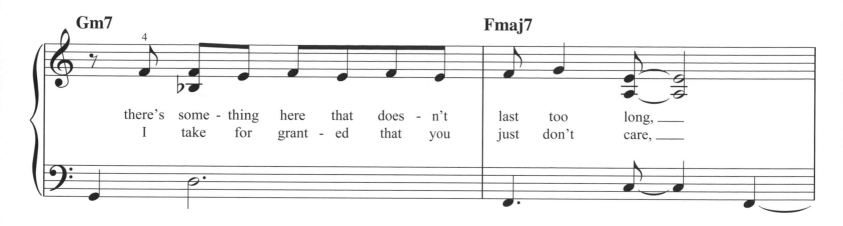

Gm7 / Fmaj7

there's some-thing here that does-n't | last too long, ___
I take for grant-ed that you | just don't care, ___

Cm7/F / Dm/F

may-be I should-n't think of | you as mine. ___
some-times I can't help see-ing | all the way through. _

Ebmaj7/F Fmaj7 / Ebmaj7/F Fmaj7 / Dm7 / Cmaj7

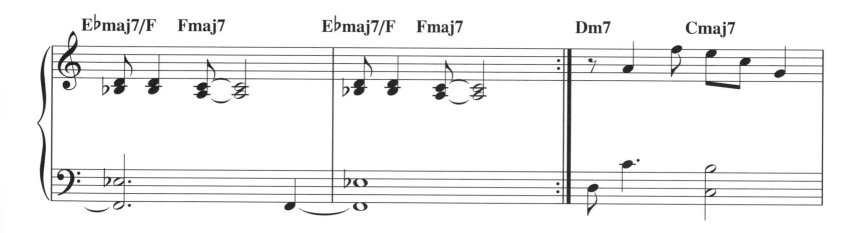

Dm7 / Cmaj7 / Bbmaj7 Fmaj7/A / Bbmaj7 Fmaj7/A

It's im-por-tant to | me _____ | that you know you are

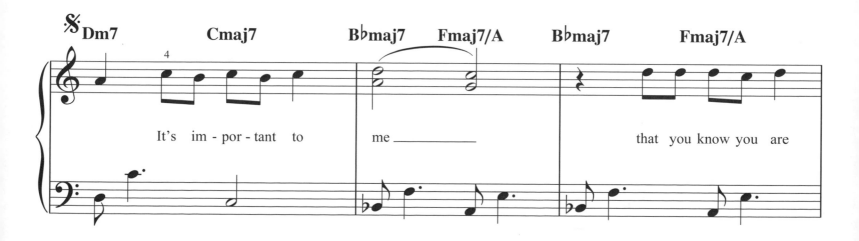

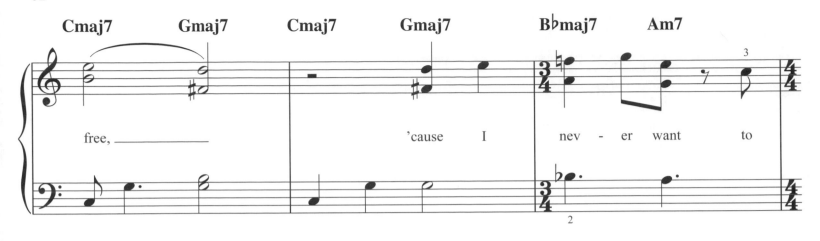

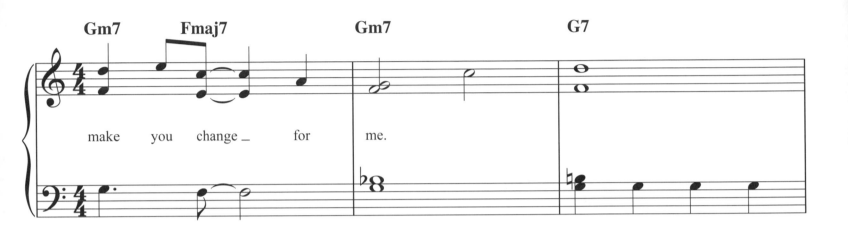

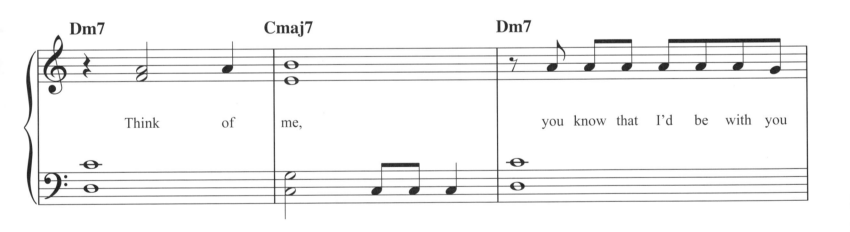

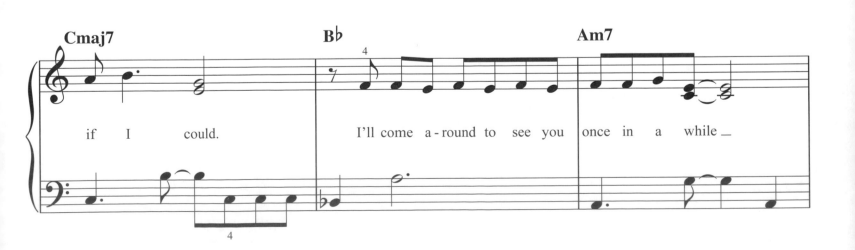

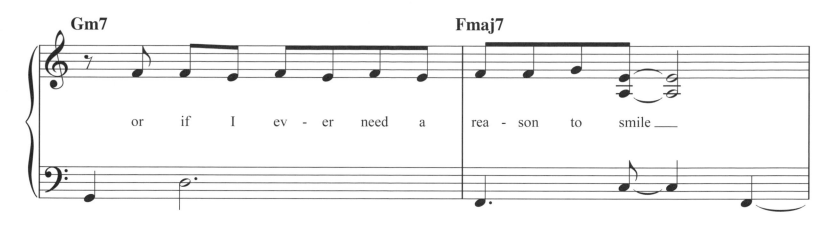

or if I ev - er need a rea - son to smile ___

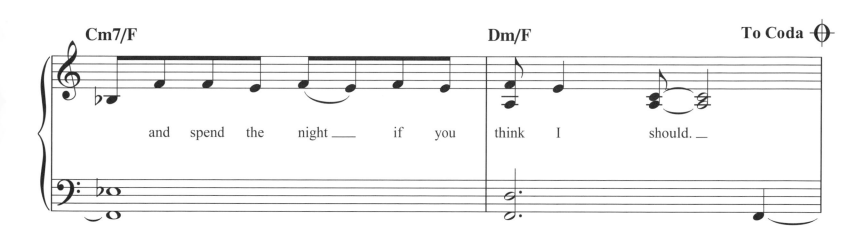

and spend the night ___ if you think I should. ___

To Coda ⊕

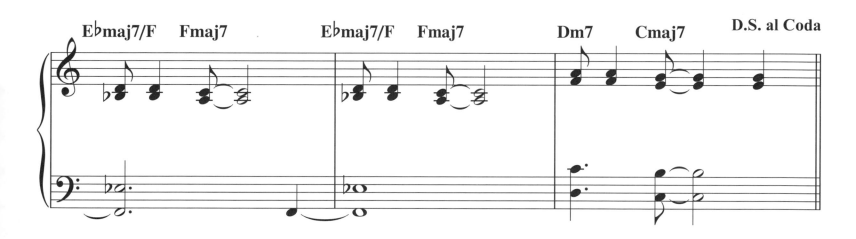

D.S. al Coda

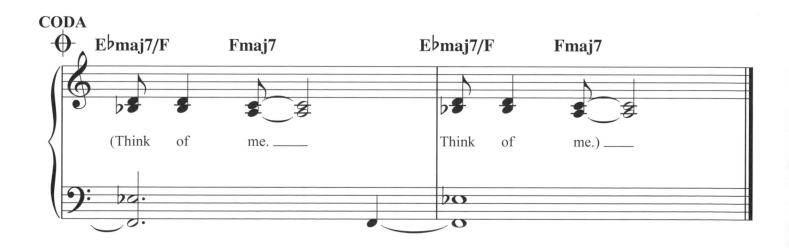

(Think of me. ___ Think of me.) ___

HEY JUDE

Words and Music by JOHN LENNON
and PAUL McCARTNEY

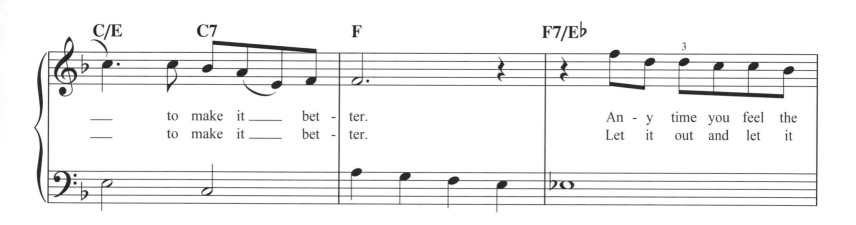

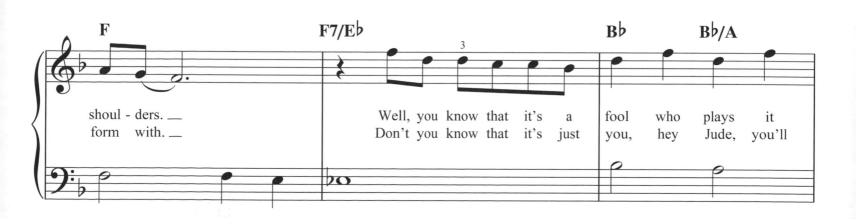

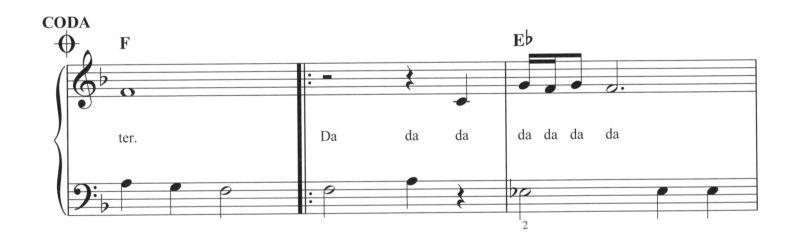

IN YOUR EYES

Words and Music by
PETER GABRIEL

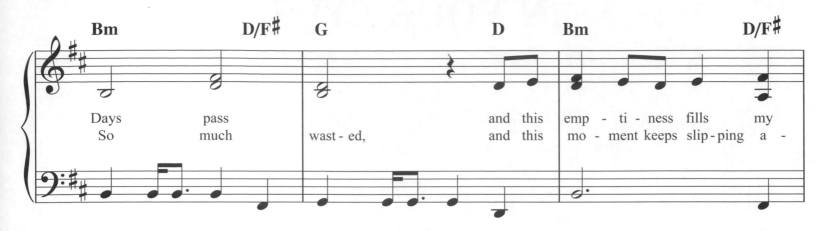

Days   pass,   and this   emp - ti - ness fills   my
So   much   wast - ed,   and this   mo - ment keeps slip - ping a -

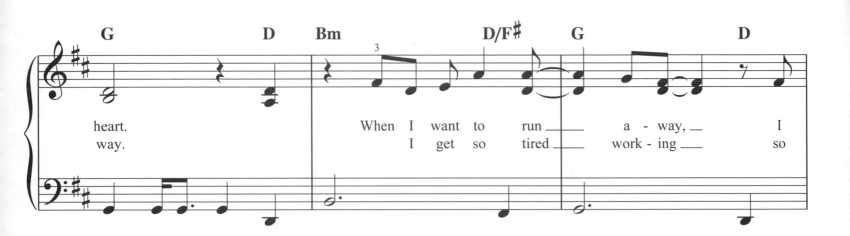

heart.   When I   want   to   run ____ a - way, ___ I
way.   I   get   so   tired ____ work - ing ___ so

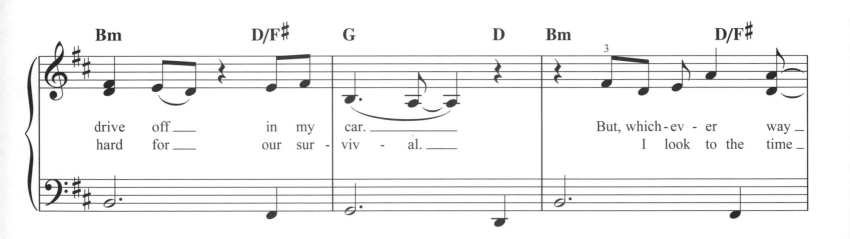

drive   off ___   in my   car. ____   But, which - ev - er   way ___
hard   for ___   our sur - viv - al. ____   I   look to the time _

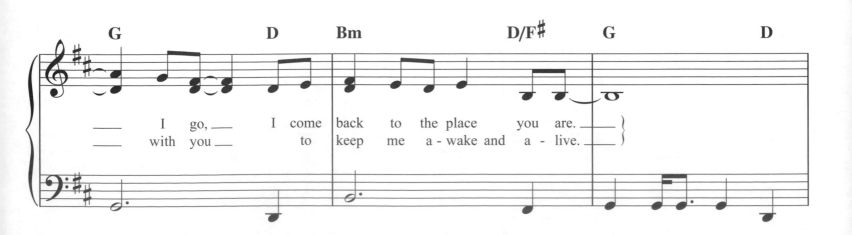

____   I   go, ___   I come back   to   the place   you are. ____
____   with you ___   to   keep   me a - wake and   a - live. ____

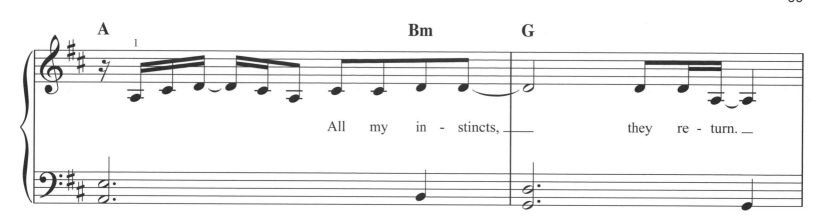

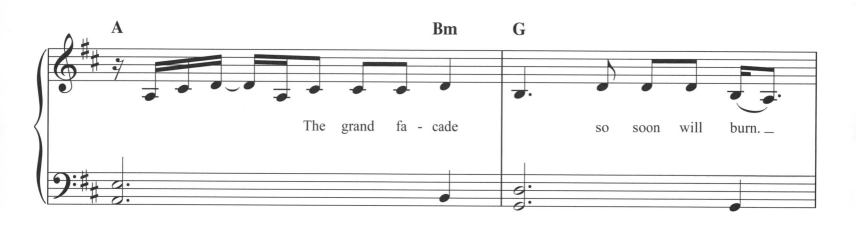

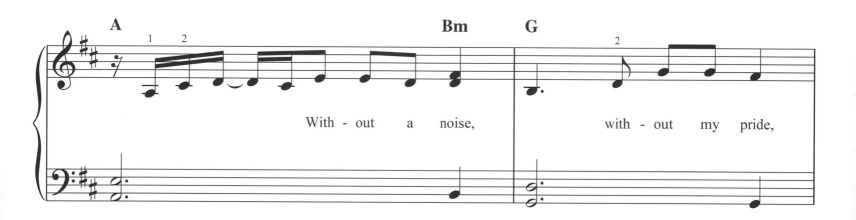

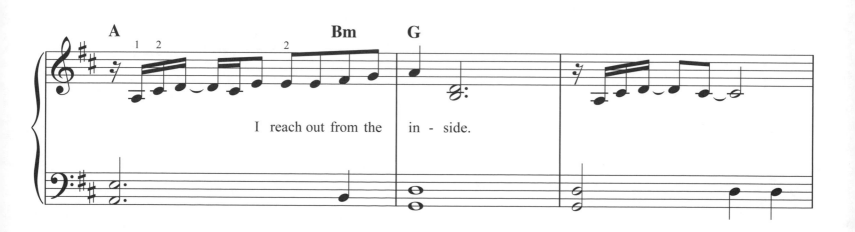

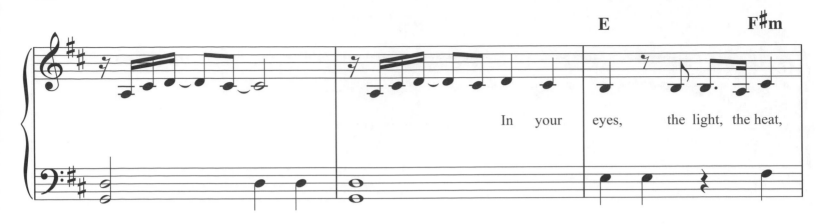

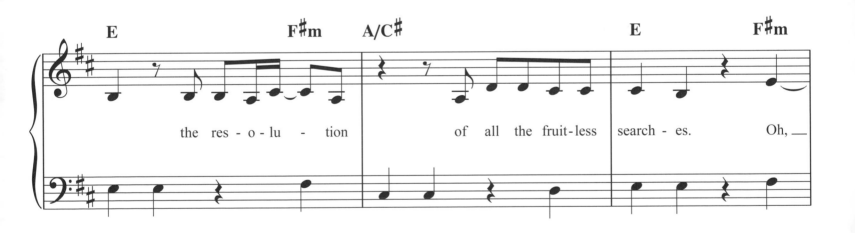

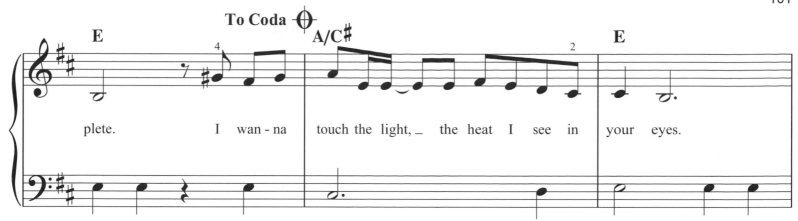

plete. I wan-na touch the light, _ the heat I see in your eyes.

touch the light, _ the heat I see in your eyes, in

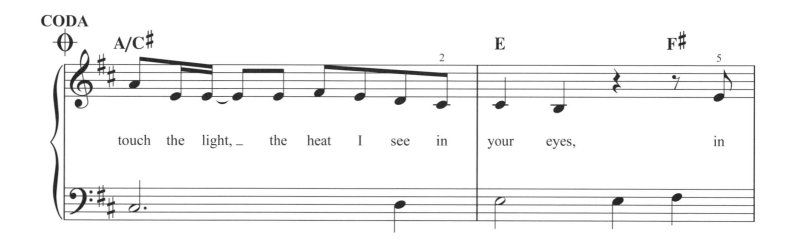

your eyes, in your eyes, in your eyes, in your eyes.

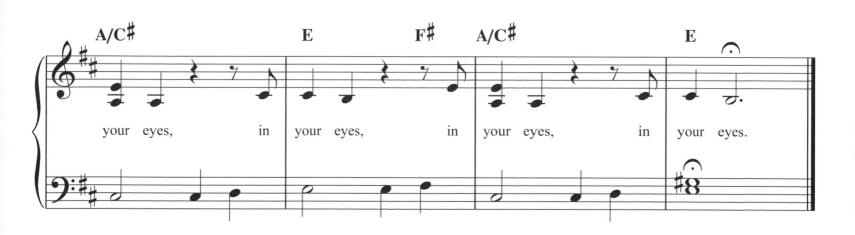

IT'S TOO LATE

Words and Music by CAROLE KING
and TONI STERN

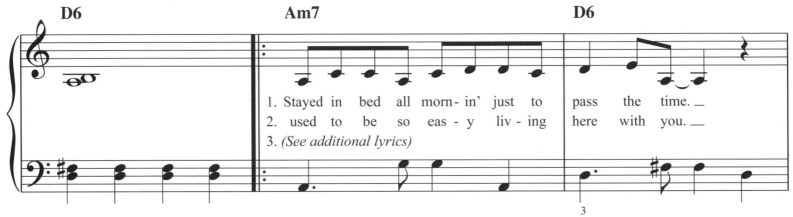

1. Stayed in bed all morn - in' just to pass the time. __
2. used to be so eas - y liv - ing here with you. __
3. *(See additional lyrics)*

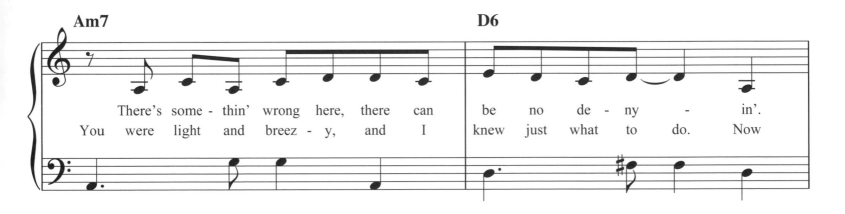

There's some - thin' wrong here, there can be no de - ny - in'.
You were light and breez - y, and I knew just what to do. Now

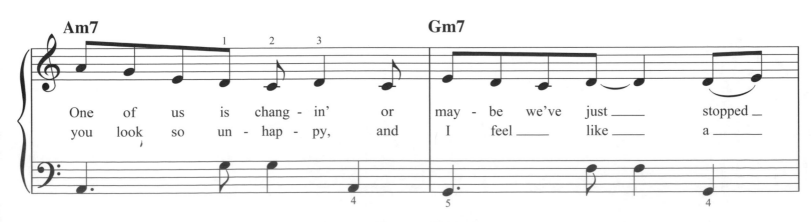

One of us is chang - in' or may - be we've just ____ stopped ____
you look so un - hap - py, and I feel ____ like ____ a

Fmaj7

Chorus

Bbmaj7

try - in'. }
fool. ____ }

And it's too late, ba - by, now ___

Fmaj7

Bbmaj7

Fmaj7

it's too late, ___ though we real - ly did ___ try to make ___ it.

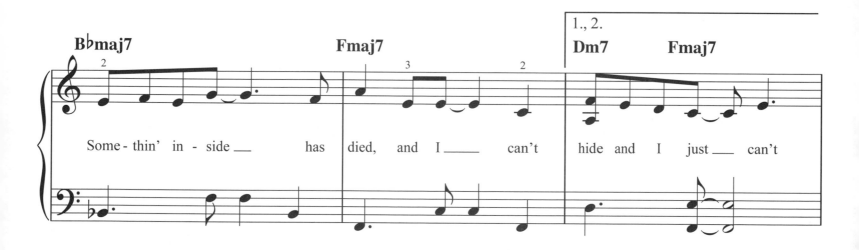

Bbmaj7

Fmaj7

1., 2.
Dm7　　Fmaj7

Some - thin' in - side ___ has died, and I ___ can't hide and I just ___ can't

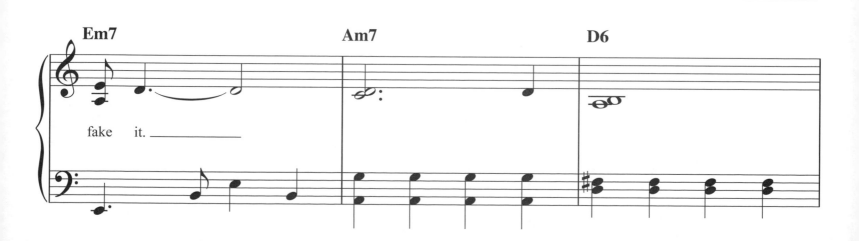

Em7

Am7

D6

fake it. _____

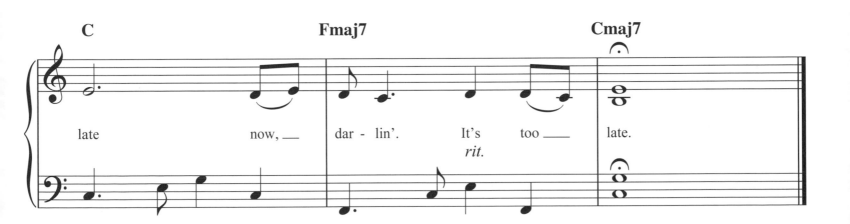

Additional Lyrics

3. There'll be good times again for me and you,
   But we just can't stay together.
   Don't you feel it, too?
   Still I'm glad for what we had
   And how I once loved you.
   Chorus

LEVON

Words and Music by ELTON JOHN
and BERNIE TAUPIN

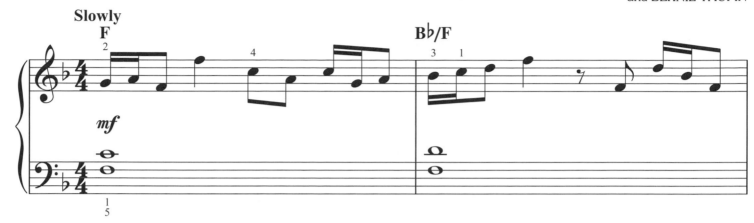

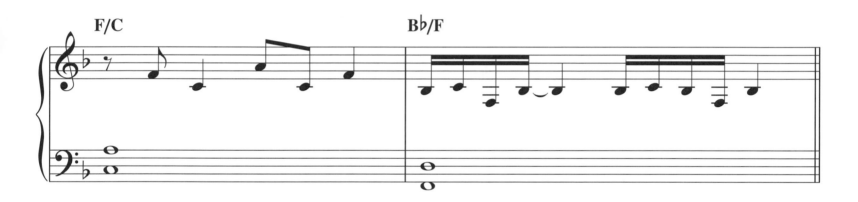

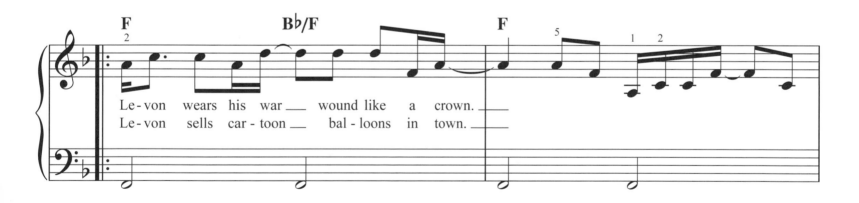

Le-von wears his war wound like a crown.
Le-von sells car-toon bal-loons in town.

He calls his child Je - sus
His fam-'ly bus'-ness thrives.

'cause he likes ___ the name, ___ and he
Je - sus blows up bal - loons ___ all day, ___ sits

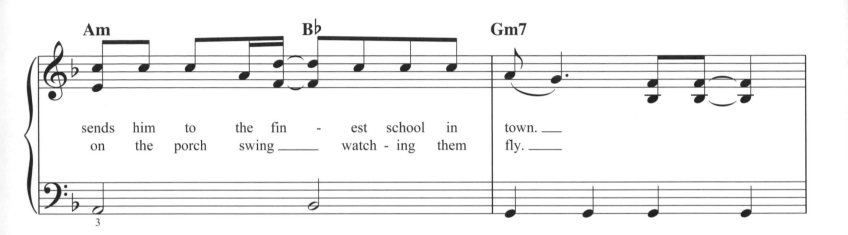

sends him to the fin - est school in town. ___
on the porch swing ___ watch - ing them fly. ___

Le - von, ___ Le - von likes his mon - ey.
Je - sus, he wants to go to Ve - nus,

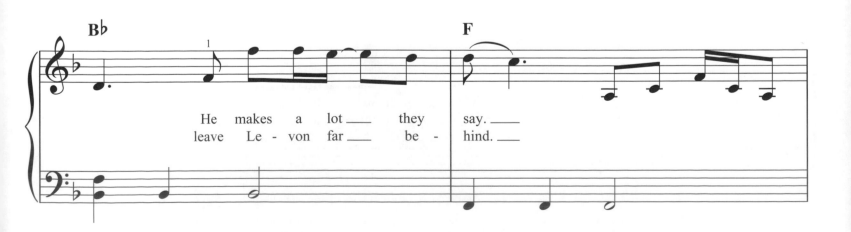

He makes a lot ___ they say. ___
leave Le - von far ___ be - hind. ___

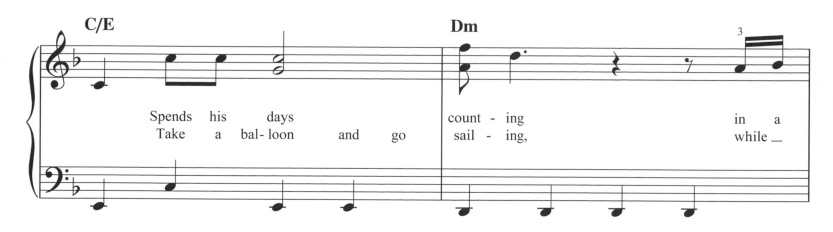

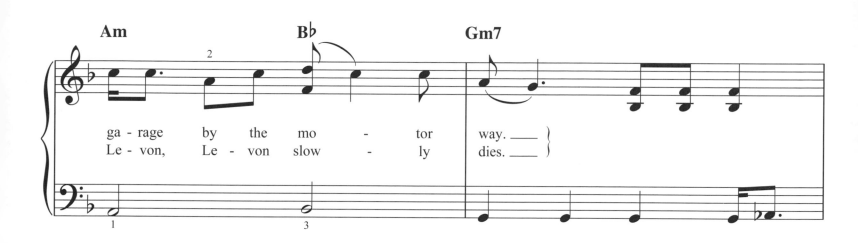

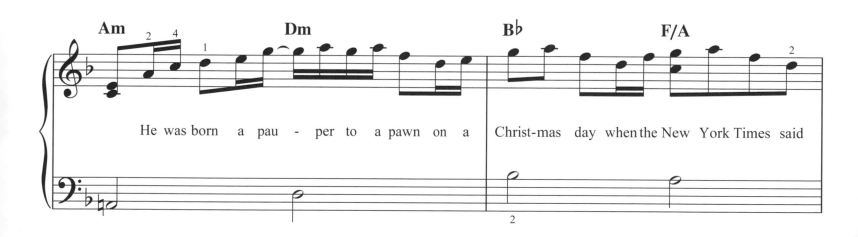

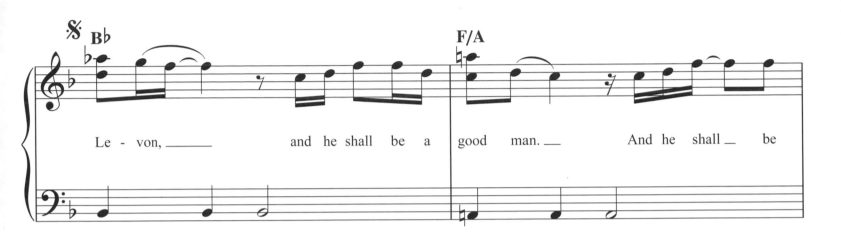

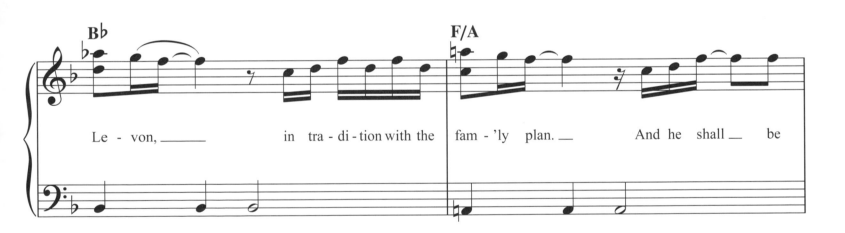

He shall __ be Le - von.

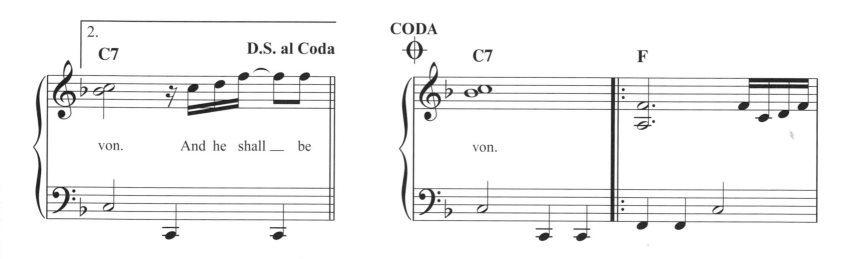

von.   And he shall __ be

von.

THE JOKER

Words and Music by STEVE MILLER,
EDDIE CURTIS and AHMET ERTEGUN

Moderately slow

Some peo-ple call me the Space Cow-boy, yeah. ____

____ Some call me the Gang-ster of Love. __ Some peo-ple call me Maur-

ice 'cause I speak of the pom-pa-tus of love. __

Peo-ple talk ___ a-bout ___ me, ba-by, say I'm do-ing you wrong, do-

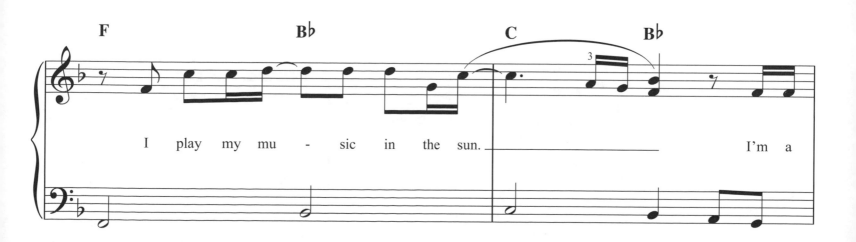

joker. I'm a smok-er. I'm a mid-night tok - er. I get my lov - ing on the run._

_ Oo, hoo. _ Oo, hoo. _

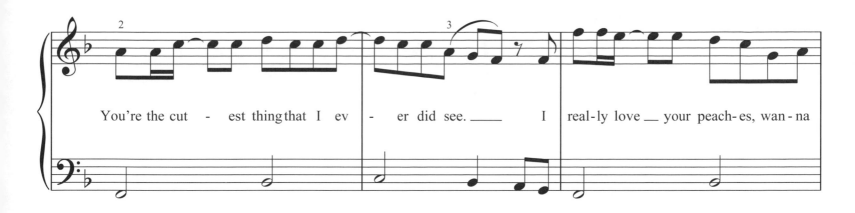

You're the cut - est thing that I ev - er did see. ____ I real-ly love __ your peach-es, wan-na

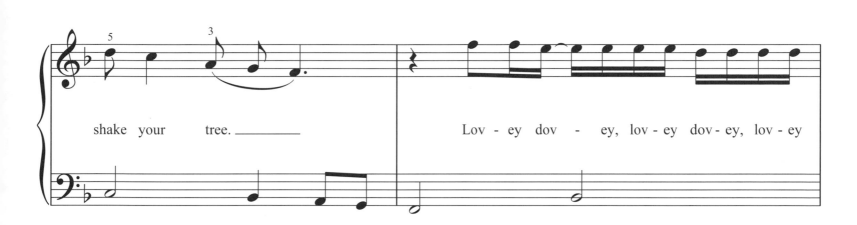

shake your tree. _____ Lov - ey dov - ey, lov - ey dov - ey, lov - ey

dov - ey all the time. _____ Oo, wee, ba - by, I'll sure show

you a good time. __ 'Cause I'm a pick - er. I'm a grin - ner. I'm a

lov-er and I'm a sin-ner. I play my mu-sic in the sun.

I'm a jok-er. I'm a smok-er. I'm a mid-night tok - er.

I sure don't wan - na hurt no one.

2.
C

Oo, hoo._____ Oo, hoo._____

N.C.

Peo - ple keep talk- in' a - bout me, ba - by. They say I'm do-ing you

wrong._____ Well, don't you wor- ry. Don't wor- ry. No, don't wor-ry, Ma - ma,

'cause I'm right here at home._____

JUMP

Words and Music by EDWARD VAN HALEN,
ALEX VAN HALEN and DAVID LEE ROTH

Driving Rock

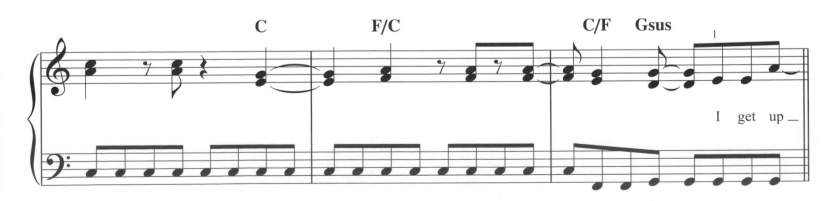

I get up

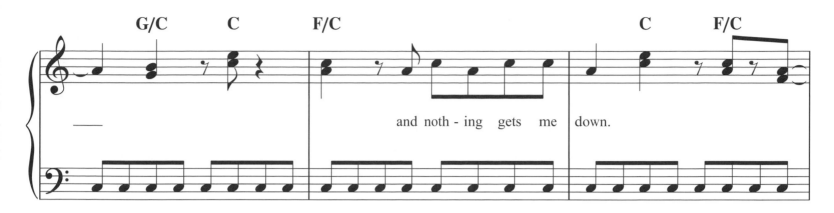

and noth - ing gets me down.

You got it tough.

I seen the tough - est soul a - round. __

And I know,

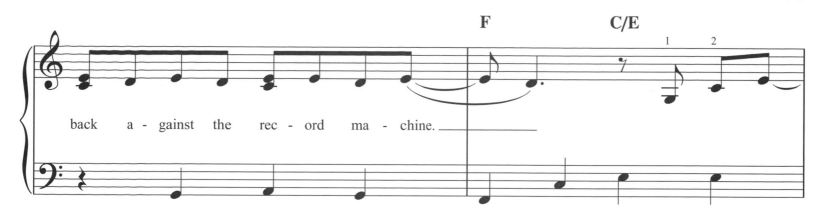

back a - gainst the rec - ord ma - chine.

I ain't the worst that you've seen.

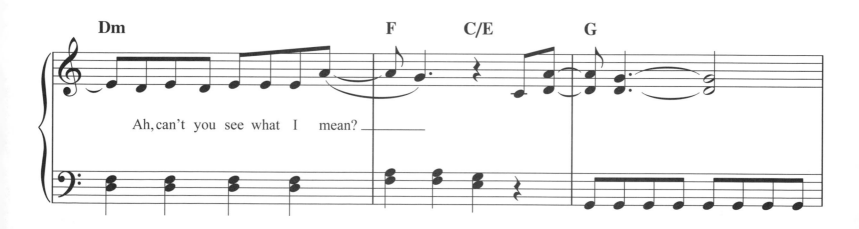

Ah, can't you see what I mean?

To Coda ⊕

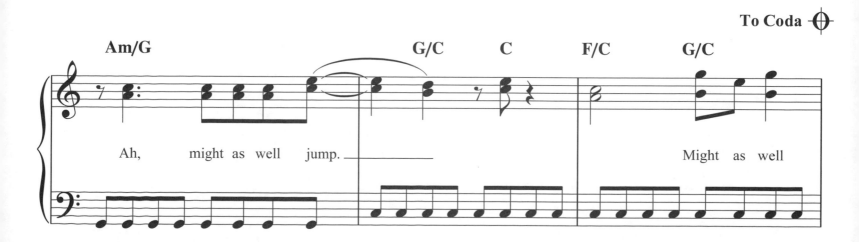

Ah, might as well jump. _____ Might as well

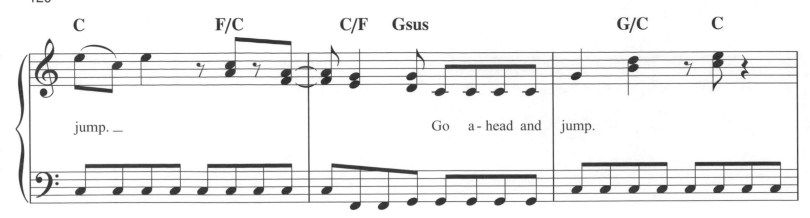

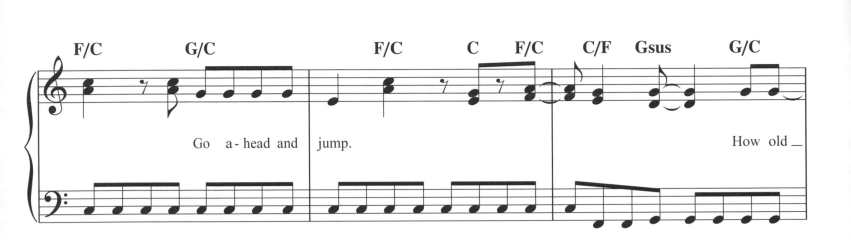

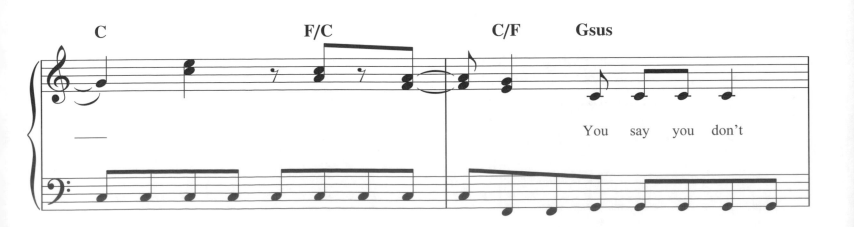

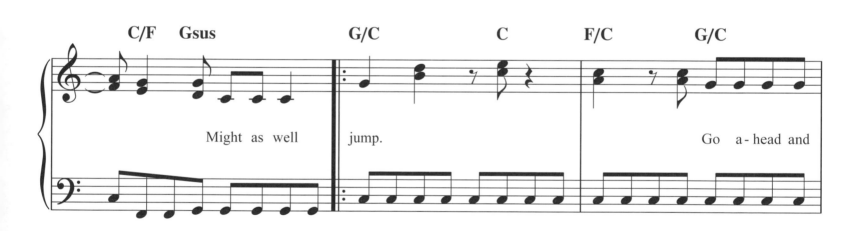

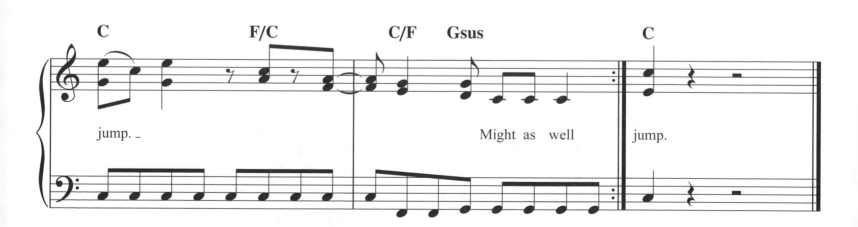

Kiss On My List

Words and Music by JANNA ALLEN
and DARYL HALL

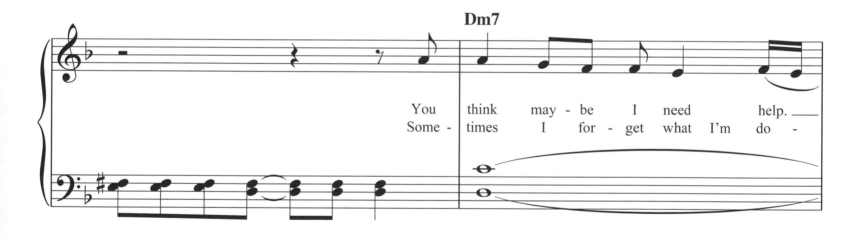

124

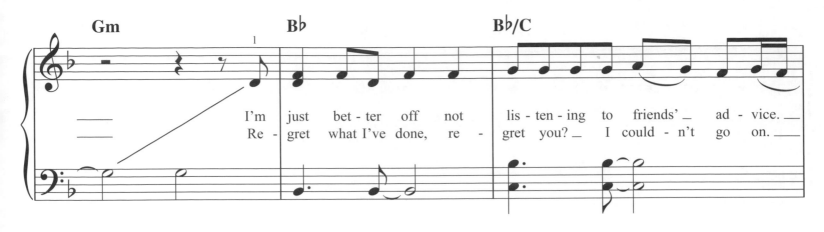

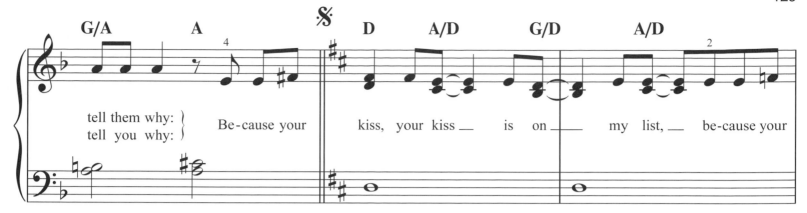

tell them why: }
tell you why: } Be-cause your kiss, your kiss ___ is on ___ my list, ___ be-cause your

kiss, your kiss, ___ is on ___ my list, ___ be-cause your kiss is on ___ my list

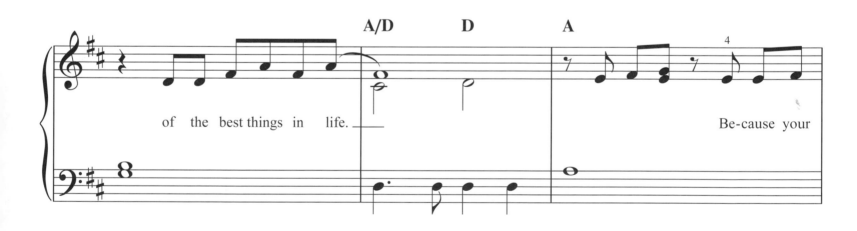

of the best things in life. ___ Be-cause your

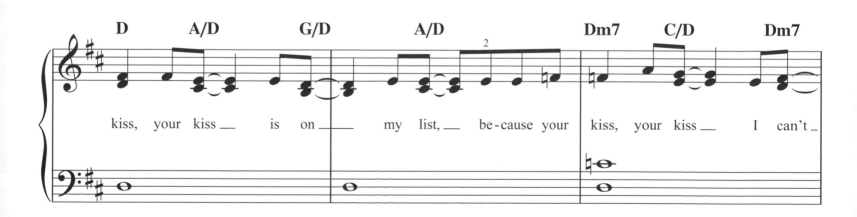

kiss, your kiss ___ is on ___ my list, ___ be-cause your kiss, your kiss ___ I can't ___

To Coda

re - sist, be-cause your kiss, is what __ I miss when I turn out the light. __

I go

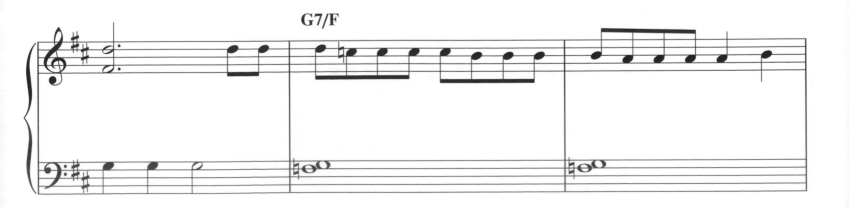

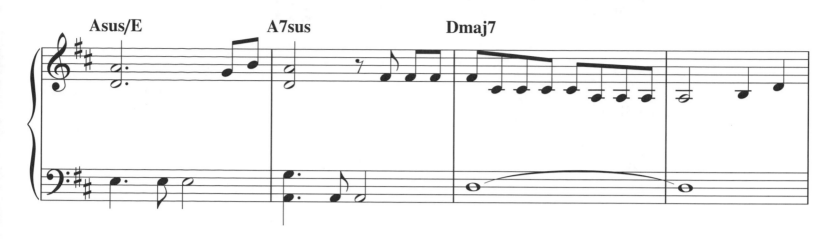

Be - cause your

LISTEN TO YOUR HEART

Words and Music by PER GESSLE
and MATS PERSSON

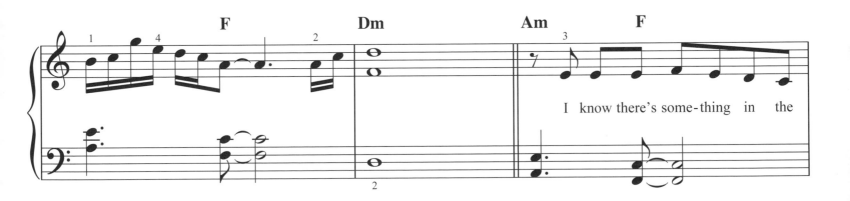

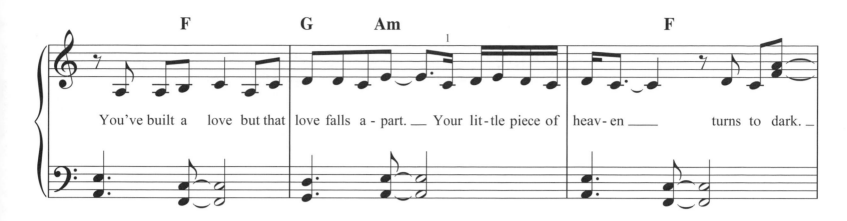

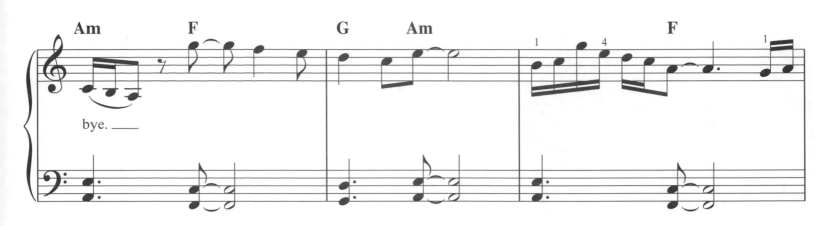

bye. ____

Some-times you won-der if this fight is worth-while. ___

The pre-cious mo-ments are all lost in the tide, ___ yeah. __ They're swept a - way and noth-ing

is what it seems. ___ The feel-ing of be- long-ing to your dreams. _____ Lis-ten to your

CODA

you tell him good - bye.

And there are voic - es   that

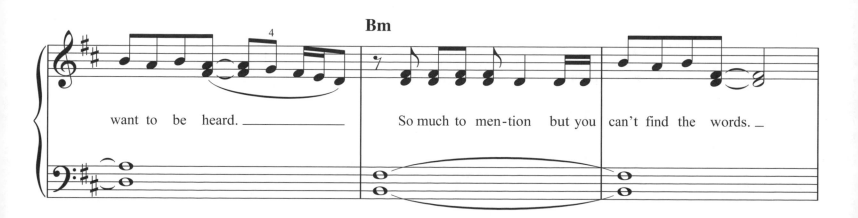

want to be heard. _____   So much to men-tion but you can't find the words. _

The scent of mag-ic. The beau-ty that's been ___ when love was wild-er ___

than the wind. ___ Lis-ten to your heart ___ when he's call-ing for you. ___ Lis-ten to your

heart, ___ there's noth-ing else you can _ do. ___ I don't know where you're go - ing and

I don't know why, ___ but lis-ten to your heart ___ be - fore... ___ Lis-ten to your

133

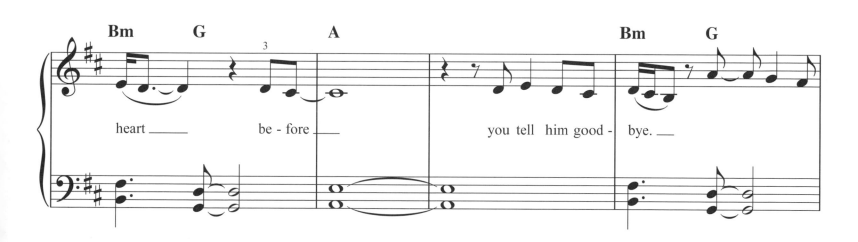

THE LOGICAL SONG

Words and Music by RICK DAVIES
and ROGER HODGSON

Moderate Rock

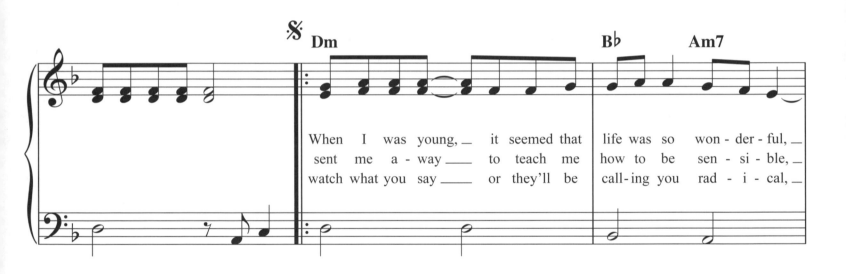

When I was young, __ it seemed that life was so won-der-ful, __
sent me a-way __ to teach me how to be sen-si-ble, __
watch what you say __ or they'll be call-ing you rad-i-cal,

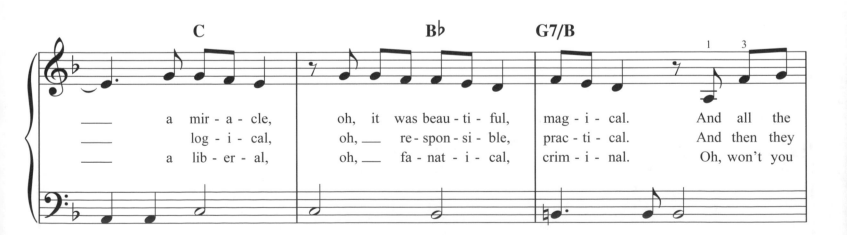

__ a mir-a-cle, oh, it was beau-ti-ful, mag-i-cal. And all the
__ log-i-cal, oh, __ re-spon-si-ble, prac-ti-cal. And then they
__ a lib-er-al, oh, __ fa-nat-i-cal, crim-i-nal. Oh, won't you

birds in the trees, ____ well, they'd be sing - ing so hap - pi - ly, ____
showed me a world ____ where I could be so de - pend - a - ble, ____
sign up your name; ____ we'd like to feel you're ac - cept - a - ble, ____

____ oh, joy - ful - ly, oh, ____ play - ful - ly
____ oh, clin - i - cal, oh, in - tel - lec - tu - al,
____ re - spect - a - ble, oh, ____ pre - sent - a - ble. A

watch - ing me. _____
cyn - i - cal. _____
veg - 'ta - ble! _____

1.
But then they

2., 3.
There are
But at

times when all the world's ____ a - sleep, the
night, when all the world's ____ a - sleep, the

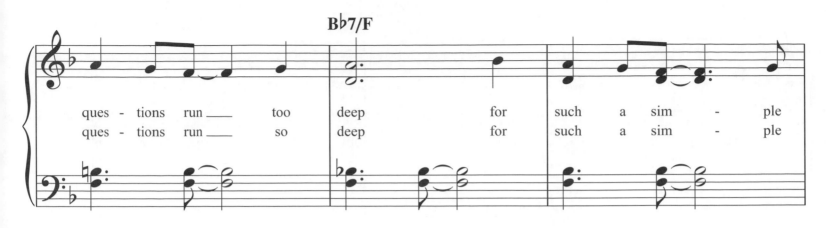

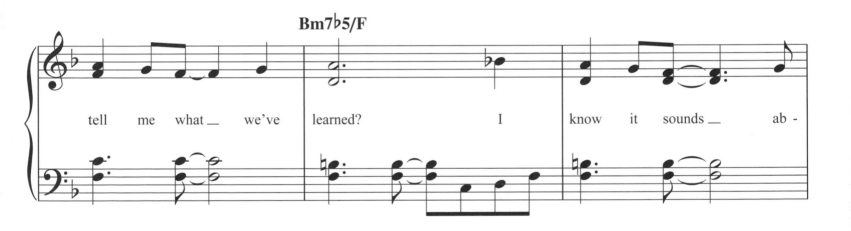

D.S. al Coda

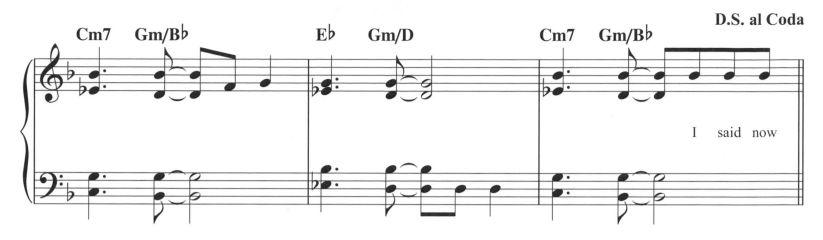

I said now

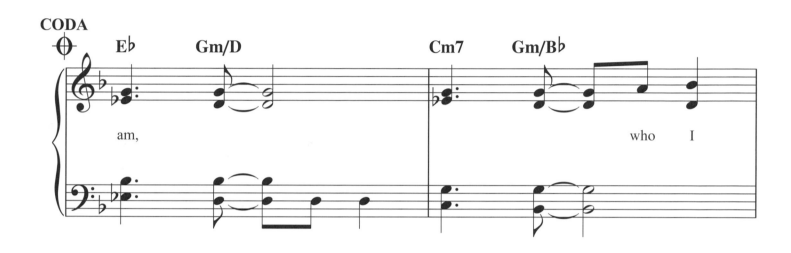

CODA

am,   who   I

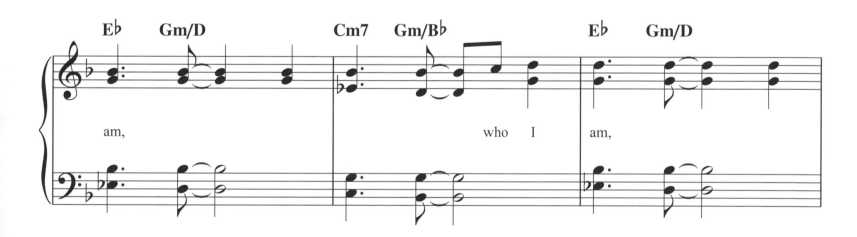

am,   who   I   am,

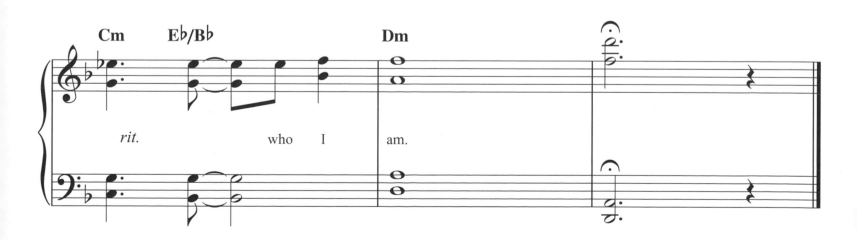

rit.   who   I   am.

MELISSA

Words and Music by GREGG ALLMAN
and STEVE ALAIMO

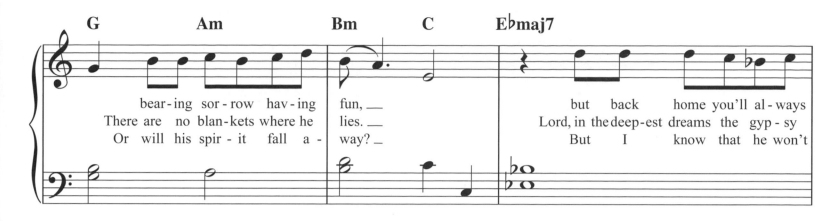

bear-ing sor-row hav-ing | fun, __ | but back home you'll al-ways
There are no blan-kets where he | lies. __ | Lord, in the deep-est dreams the gyp-sy
Or will his spir-it fall a- | way? __ | But I know that he won't

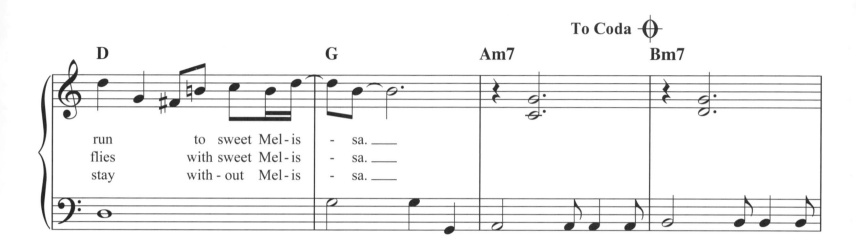

To Coda

run to sweet Mel-is - sa. __
flies with sweet Mel-is - sa. __
stay with-out Mel-is - sa. __

A-gain the morn-in's come, __ a-gain he's on the run. __

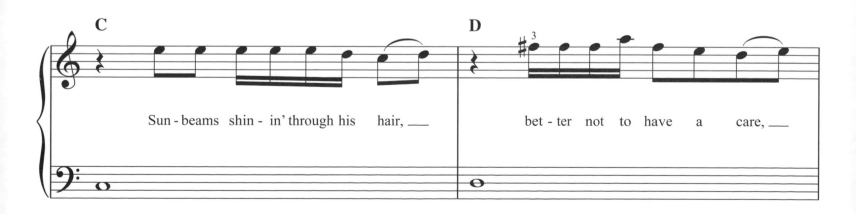

Sun-beams shin-in' through his hair, __ bet-ter not to have a care, __

so pick up your gear and gyp-sy roll ___ on, _____ roll ___ on.

D.S. al Coda

CODA

Yes, I know ___ that he won't stay, with-out Mel-

is-sa. ___ No, ___ no, he just won't stay. ___

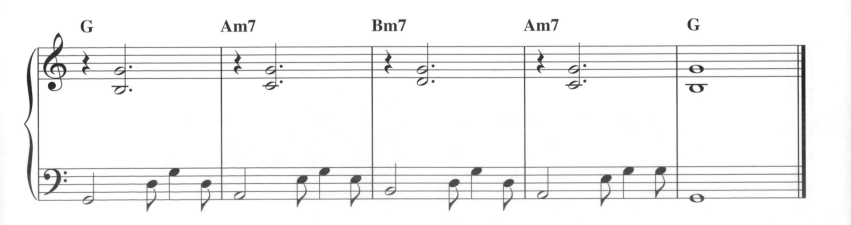

MAYBE I'M AMAZED

Words and Music by
PAUL McCARTNEY

Baby, I'm a-mazed at the way you love me all the time,
May-be I'm a-mazed at the way you're with me all the time,

and may-be I'm a-fraid of the way I love you.
and may-be I'm a-fraid of the way I need you.

May-be I'm a-mazed at the way you pulled me out of time,
May-be I'm a-mazed at the way you help me sing my song,

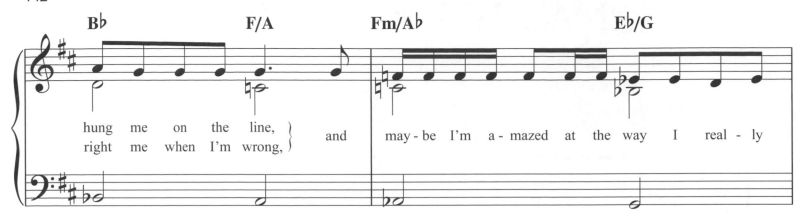

hung me on the line,
right me when I'm wrong, and may-be I'm a-mazed at the way I real-ly

need you. Ba-by, I'm a man, may-be I'm a

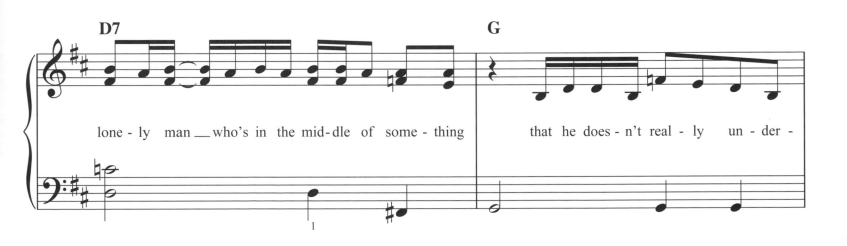

lone-ly man who's in the mid-dle of some-thing that he does-n't real-ly un-der-

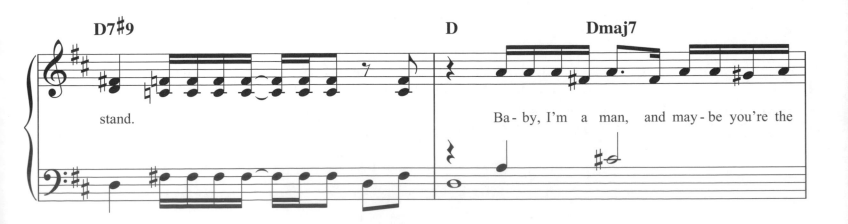

stand. Ba-by, I'm a man, and may-be you're the

only wom - an who could ev - er help me; ba - by, won't you help me to un - der -

stand? Oo. ____

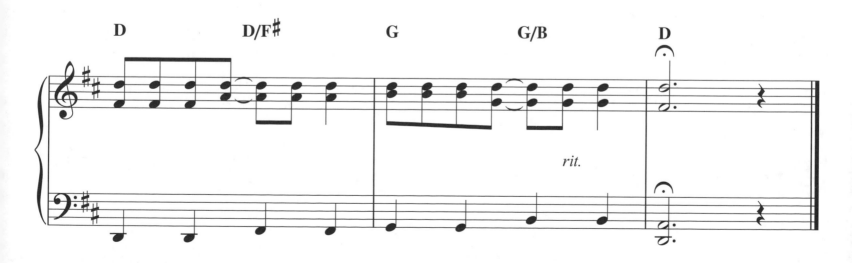

MORE THAN A FEELING

Words and Music by
TOM SCHOLZ

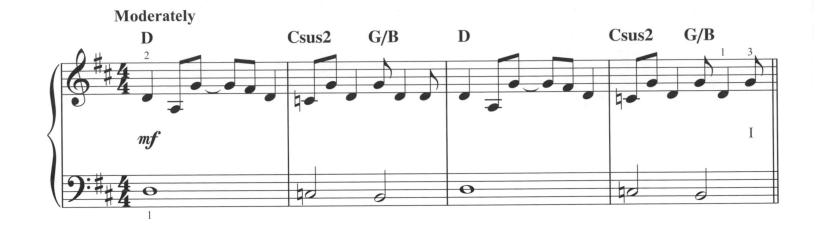

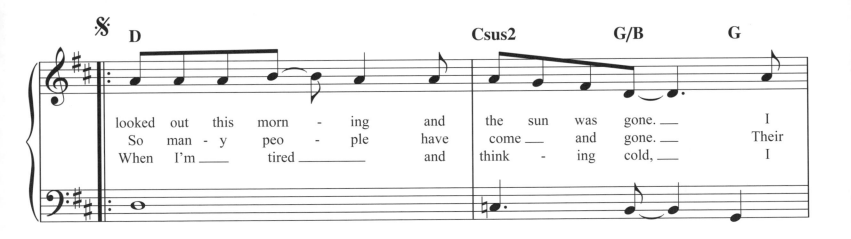

looked out this morn - ing and the sun was gone. ___ I
So man - y peo - ple have come ___ and gone. ___ Their
When I'm ___ tired ___ and think - ing cold, ___ I

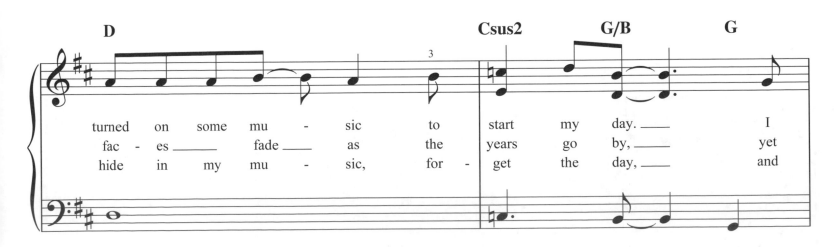

turned on some mu - sic to start my day. ___ I
fac - es ___ fade ___ as the years go by, ___ yet
hide in my mu - sic, for - get the day, ___ and

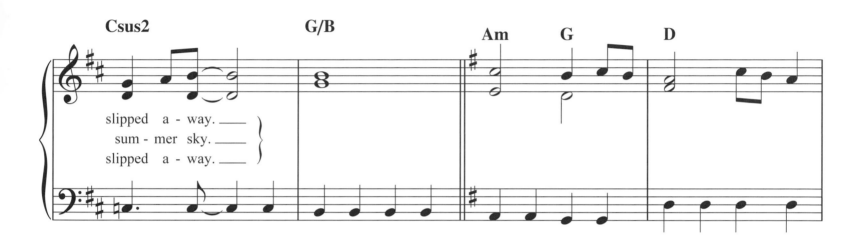

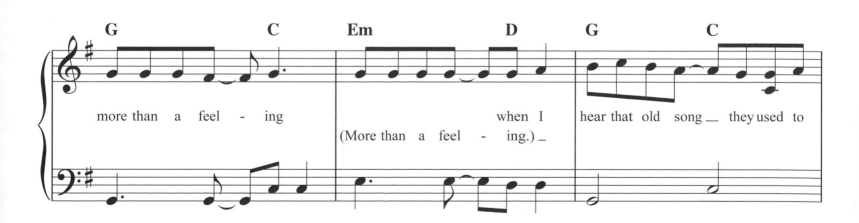

To Coda ⊕

play. _____ I be-gin dream - ing till I
(More than a feel - ing.) _ (More than a feel - ing.) _

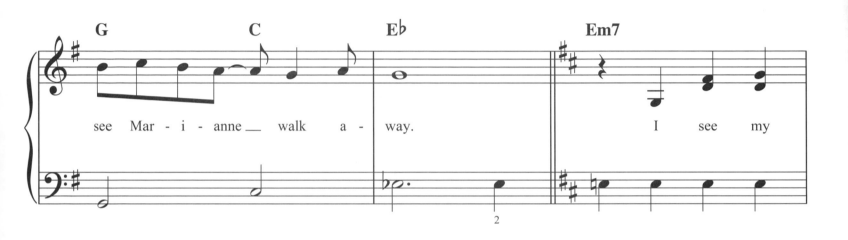

see Mar - i - anne ___ walk a - way. I see my

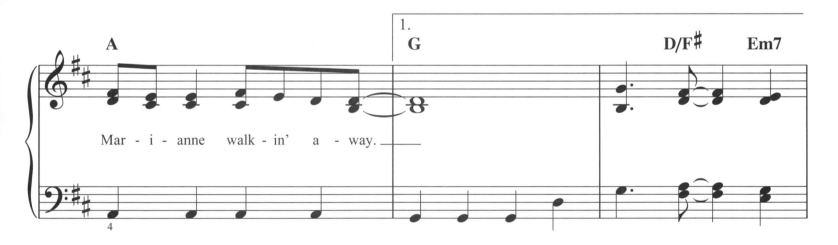

Mar - i - anne walk - in' a - way. ___

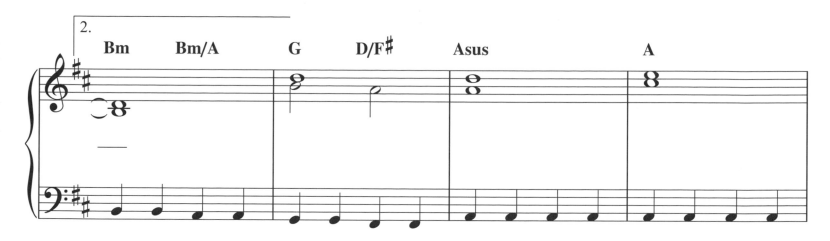

D.S. al Coda

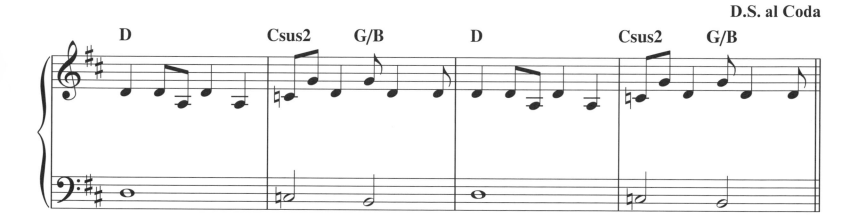

CODA

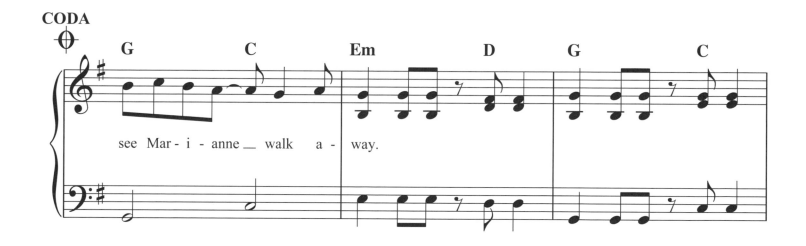

see Mar - i - anne __ walk a - way.

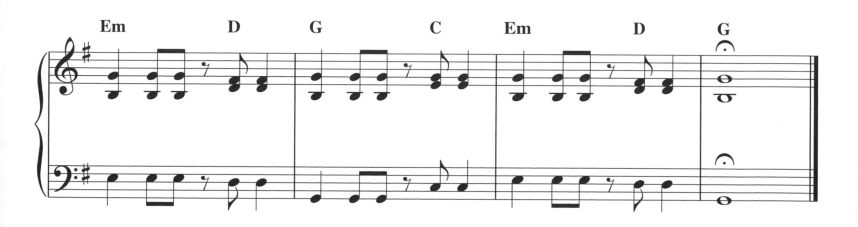

NOVEMBER RAIN

Words and Music by
W. AXL ROSE

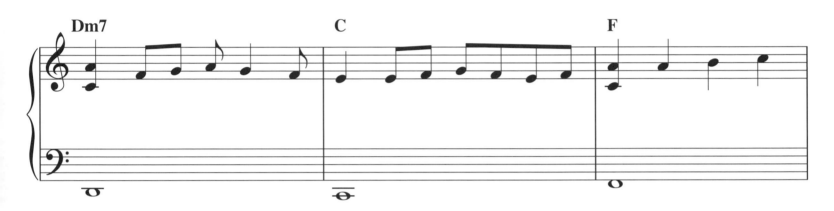

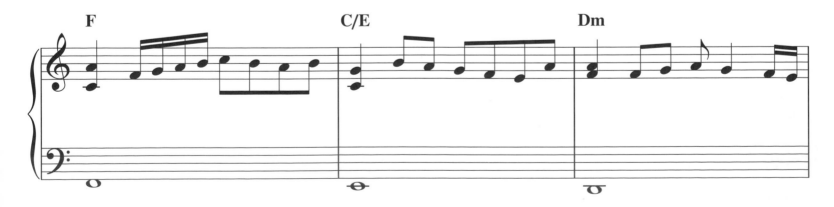

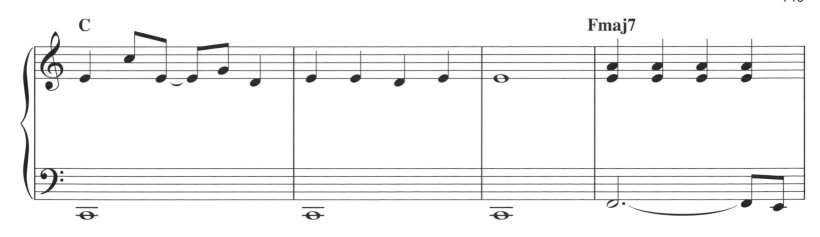

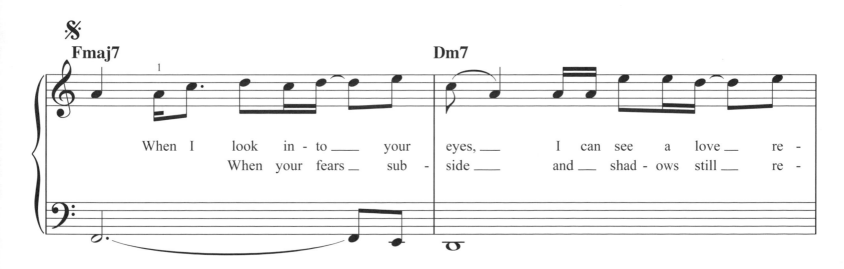

When I look in - to ____ your eyes, ____ I can see a love ____ re -
When your fears ____ sub - side ____ and ____ shad - ows still ____ re -

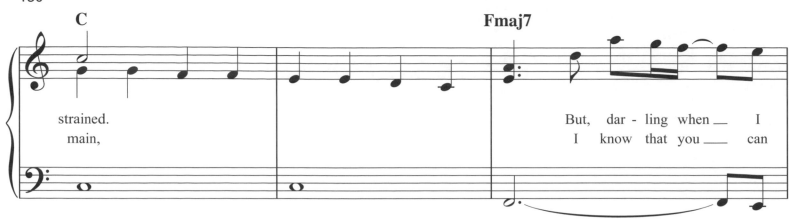

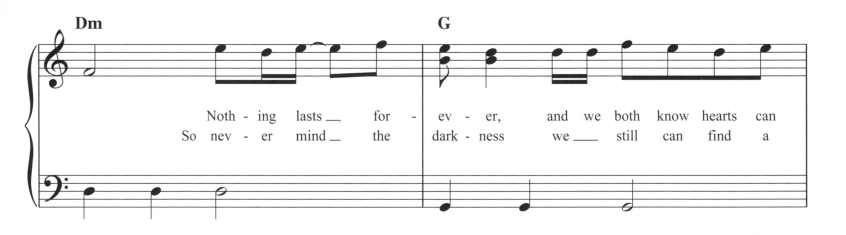

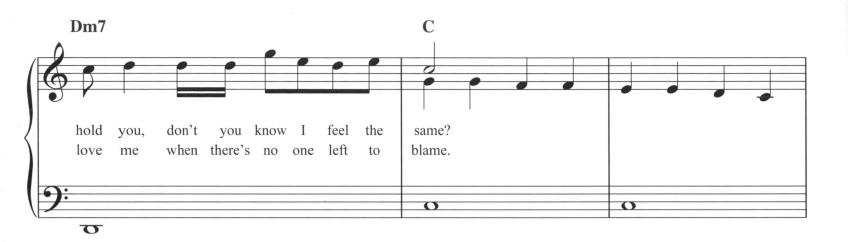

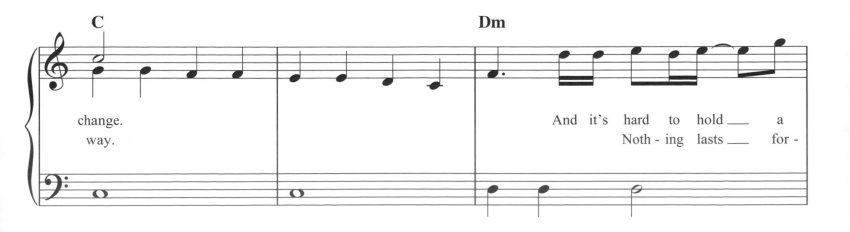

can - dle   in the   cold No - vem - ber | rain.
ev - er,   e - ven cold No - vem - ber

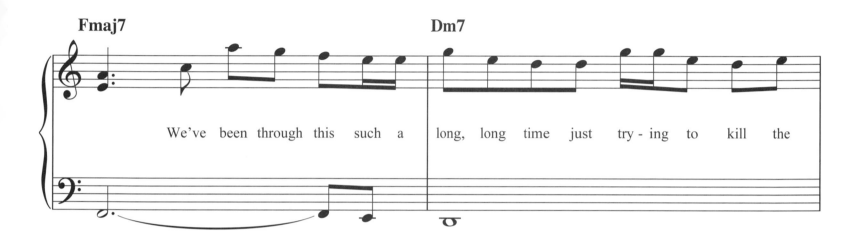

We've been through this   such a | long, long time just try - ing to kill the

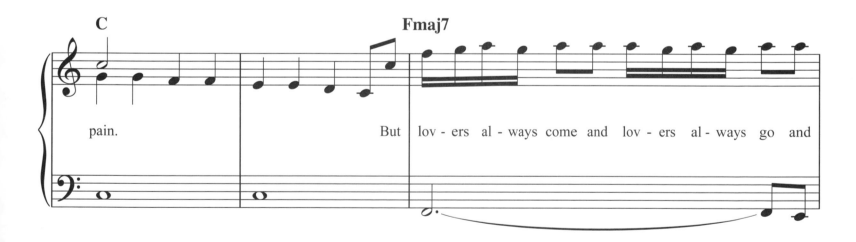

pain. | But lov - ers al - ways come and lov - ers al - ways go and

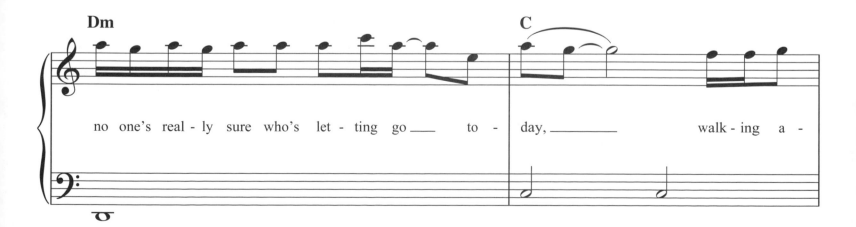

no one's real - ly sure who's let - ting go ___ to - day, ___   walk - ing a -

way. _____ If we could take the time to lay it on the line, I could

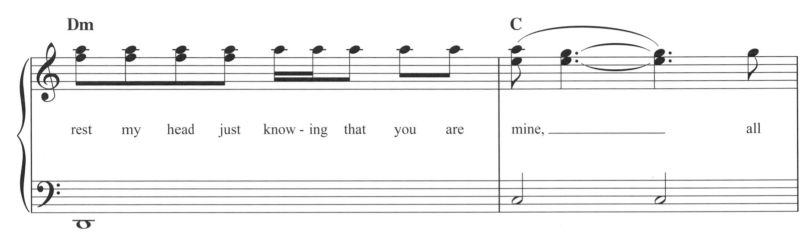

rest my head just know-ing that you are mine, _____ all

mine. _____ So if you wan - na love me, then dar - ling, don't re -

frain, or I'll just end ___ up

walk - ing   in the cold No - vem - ber   rain.   Do you

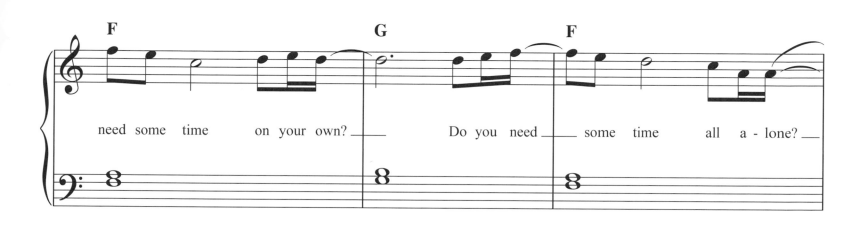

need some time   on your own? ____   Do you need ____ some time   all a - lone? ____

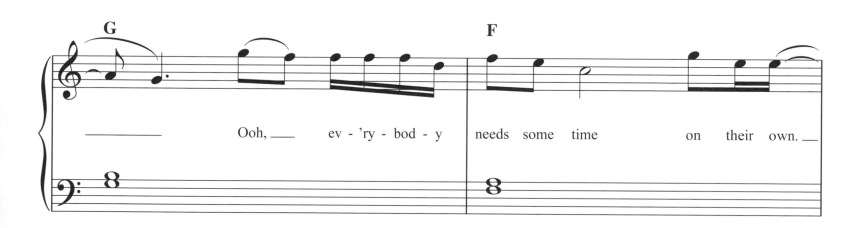

____   Ooh, ____ ev - 'ry - bod - y   needs some time   on their own. ____

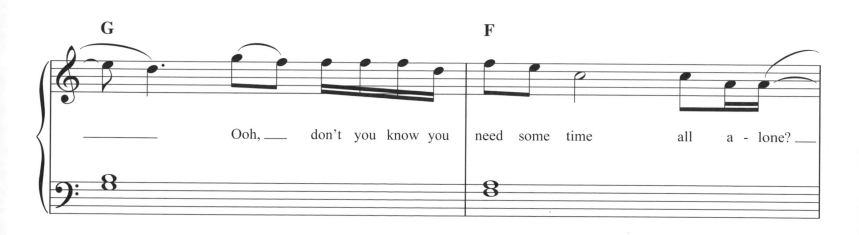

____   Ooh, ____ don't you know you   need some time   all a - lone? ____

I know it's hard __ to keep __ an o - pen heart __

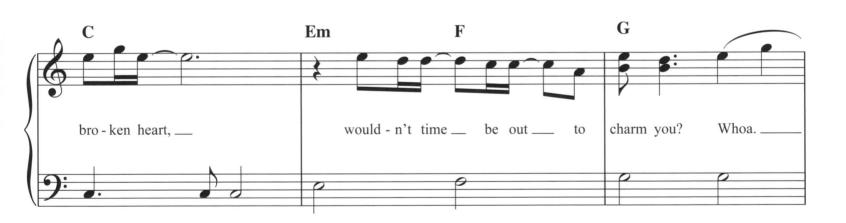

when e - ven friends __ seem out __ to harm you. But if you __ could heal __ a

bro - ken heart, __ would - n't time __ be out __ to charm you? Whoa. __

_____ Some-times I need some time on my own. __ Some - times I need __

some time   all a - lone.   Ooh, __ ev - 'ry - bod - y   needs some time   on their own. __

Ooh, __ don't you know you   need some time   all a - lone? __   **D.S. al Coda**

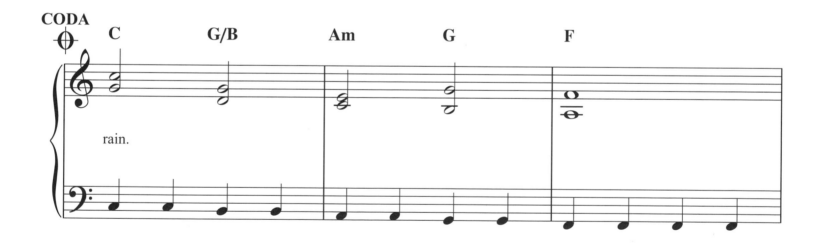

CODA
rain.

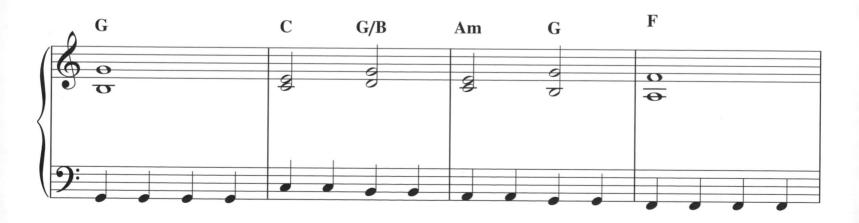

THE SEARCH IS OVER

Words and Music by JAMES M. PETERIK
and FRANK SULLIVAN

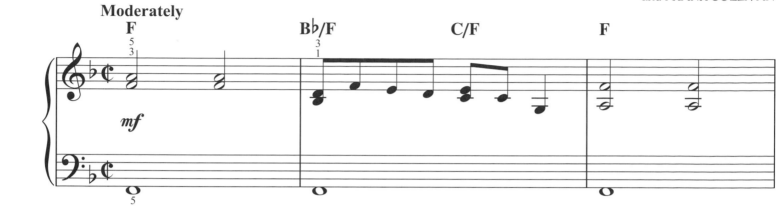

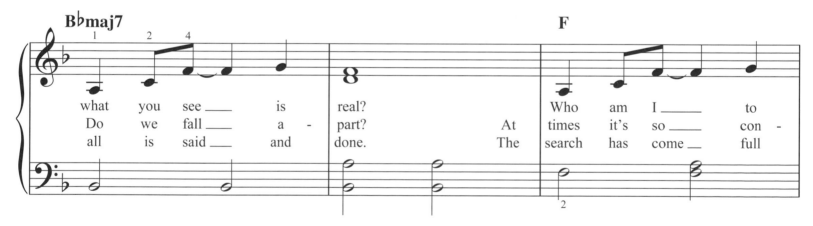

How can I _____ con - vince you
Can we last _____ for - ev - er?
Now at last _____ I hold you. Now

what you see ____ is real? Who am I _____ to
Do we fall ____ a - part? At times it's so ____ con -
all is said ____ and done. The search has come ____ full

blame you for doubt - ing what you feel? You
fus - ing, the ques - tions of the heart. So
cir - cle; our des - ti - nies are one.

I was al - ways reach - ing.
fol - lowed me ___ through chang - es and
if you ev - er loved me,

You were just a
pa - tient - ly you'd
show me that you

girl I knew. ___ I took for grant - ed the
wait till I ___ came to my sens - es through
give a damn. ___ You'll know for cer - tain the

friend I have ___ in you.
some mir - a - cle of fate.
man I real - ly am.

I was liv - ing for

a dream, lov - ing for a mo - ment. ___ Tak - ing on

the world, that was just my style.

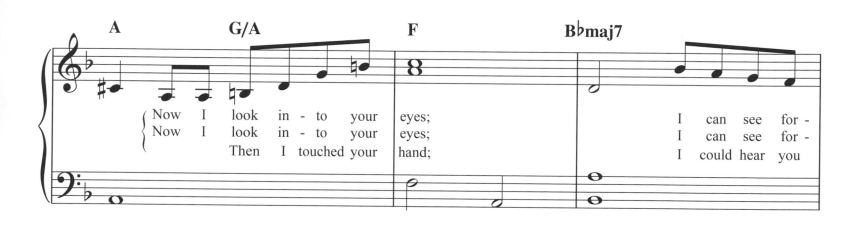

Now I look in-to your eyes; I can see for-
Now I look in-to your eyes; I can see for-
Then I touched your hand; I could hear you

ev - er. The search is o - ver. You were
ev - er. The search is o - ver. You were
whis - per. The search is o - ver. Love was

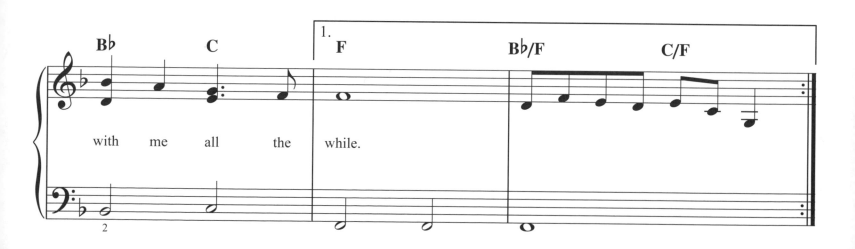

with me all the while.

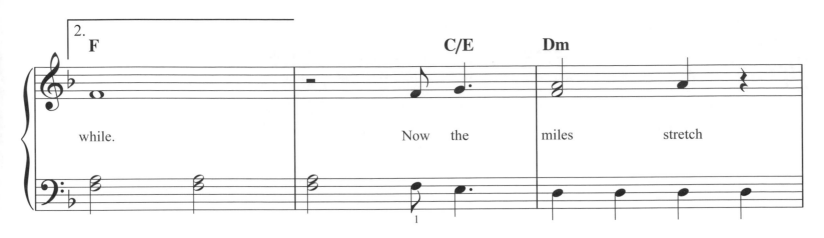

while.   Now the   miles   stretch

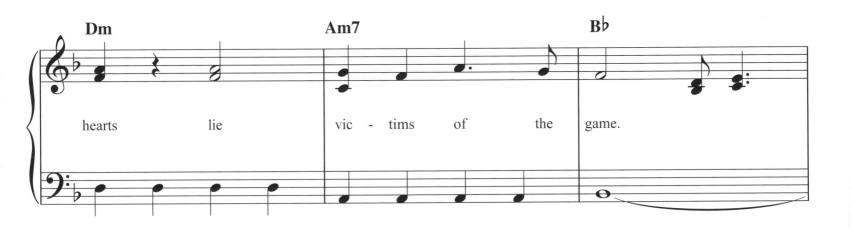

out be - hind ____ me,   loves that I ____ have   lost.   Bro - ken

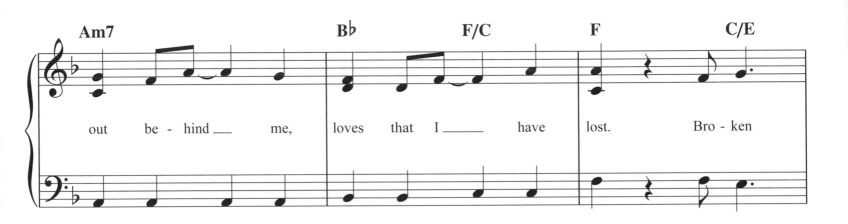

hearts   lie   vic - tims of the game.

Then   good   luck,   it   fi - n'lly struck   like

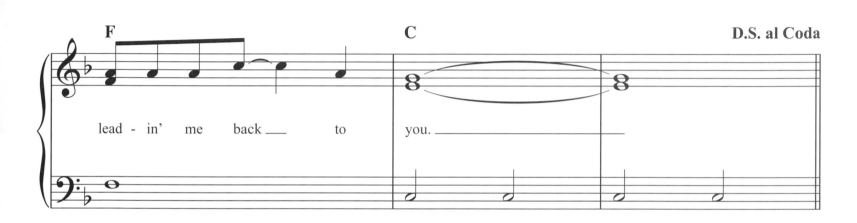

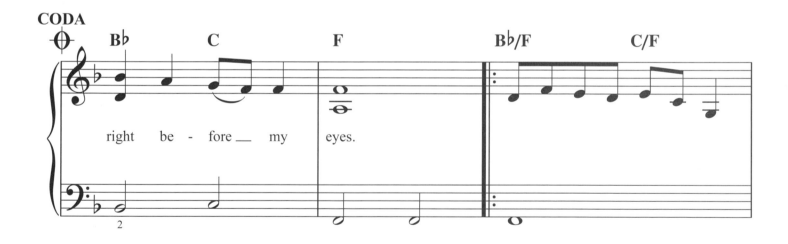

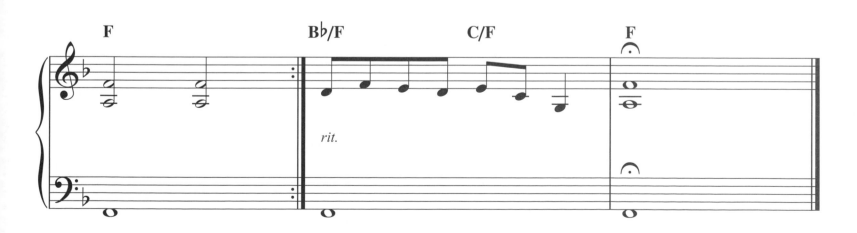

OPEN ARMS

Words and Music by STEVE PERRY
and JONATHAN CAIN

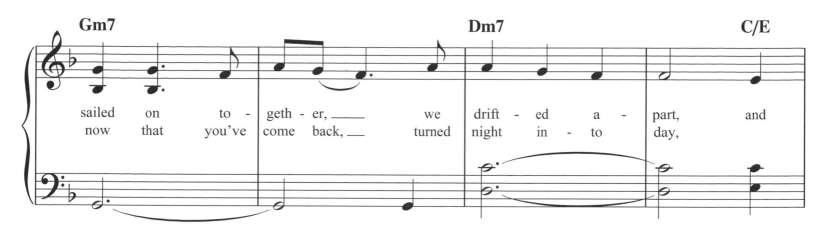

sailed on to - geth - er, _____ we drift - ed a - part, and
now that you've come back, _____ we turned night in - to day,

here you are by my side. _____
I need you to stay. _____

So _____ now I come _____ to you _____ with

o - pen _____ arms. _____ Noth - ing to hide, _____ be -

lieve what I say. _____ So here _____ I am _____ with

o - pen arms, _____ hop - ing you'll see _____ what your

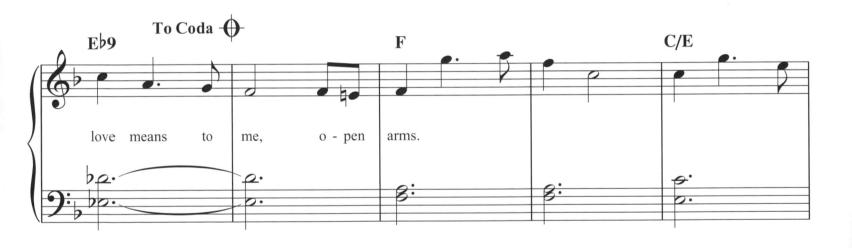

love means to me, o - pen arms.

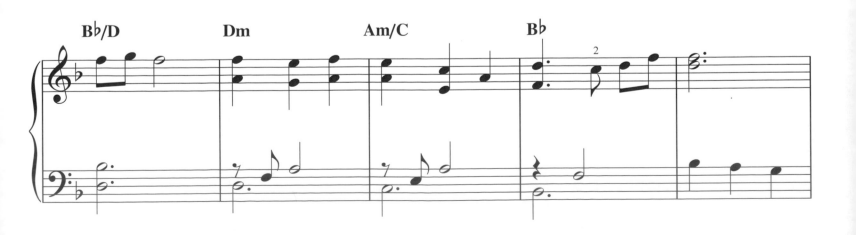

Living with- out ___ you, ___ liv-ing a - lone, ___

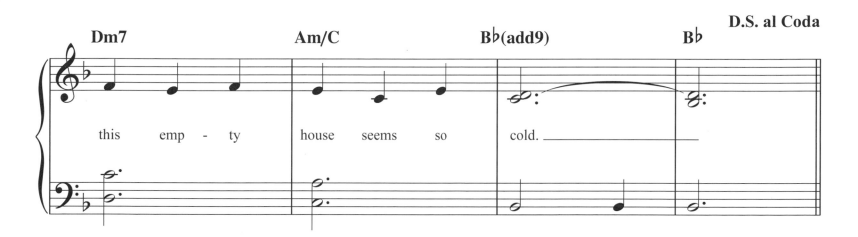

D.S. al Coda

this emp - ty house seems so cold. ___

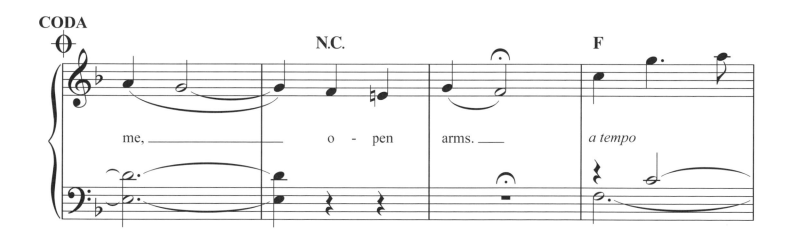

me, ___ o - pen arms. ___

a tempo

rit.

PROUD MARY

Words and Music by
JOHN FOGERTY

Moderate Rock

Left a good job ___ in the cit - y, ___
Cleaned a lot of plates in Mem - phis, ___
If you come down ___ to the riv - er, ___

work - in' for the man ___ ev - 'ry night and day. ___
pumped a lot of 'pane ___ down in New Or - leans. ___
bet you gon - na find ___ some peo - ple who live.

And I nev - er lost ___ one min - ute of sleep - in',
But I nev - er saw ___ the good side of the cit - y
You don't have to wor - ry 'cause you have no mon - ey.

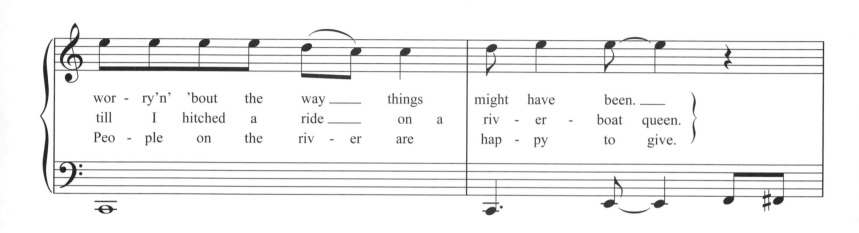

wor - ry'n' 'bout the way ___ things might have been. ___
till I hitched a ride ___ on a riv - er - boat queen.
Peo - ple on the riv - er are hap - py to give.

G   **Am**

Big wheel ___ keep on turn - in', ___ proud Mar - y keep on

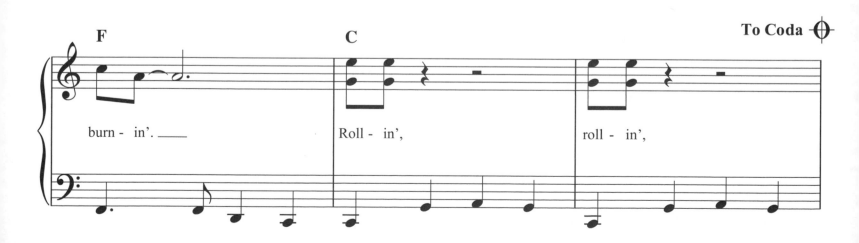

F   **C**   **To Coda** ⊕

burn - in'. ___ Roll - in', roll - in',

SHE'S ALWAYS A WOMAN

Words and Music by
BILLY JOEL

172

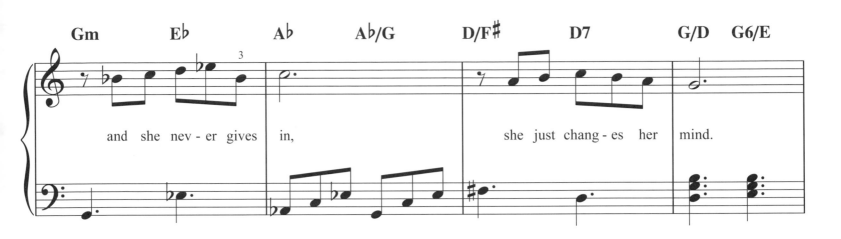

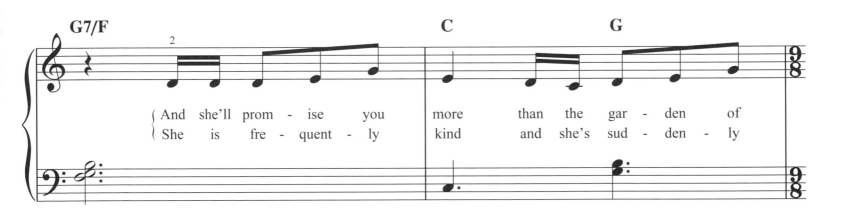

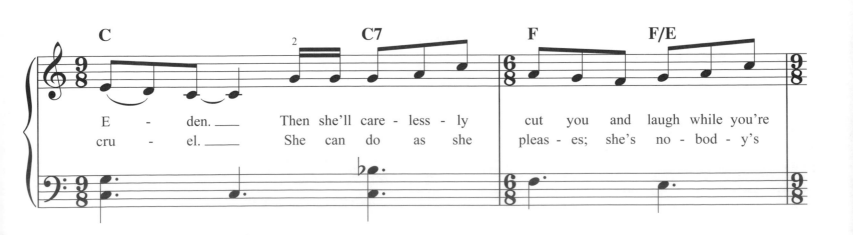

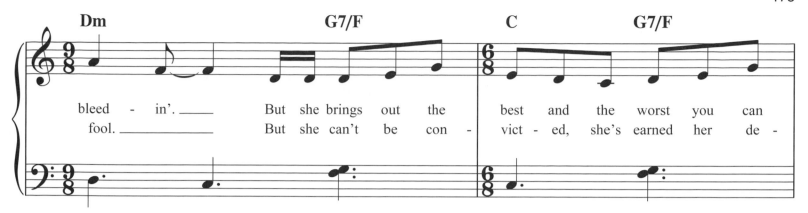

Dm   **G7/F**   **C**   **G7/F**

bleed - in'. ____ But she brings out the best and the worst you can
fool. _____ But she can't be con - vict - ed, she's earned her de -

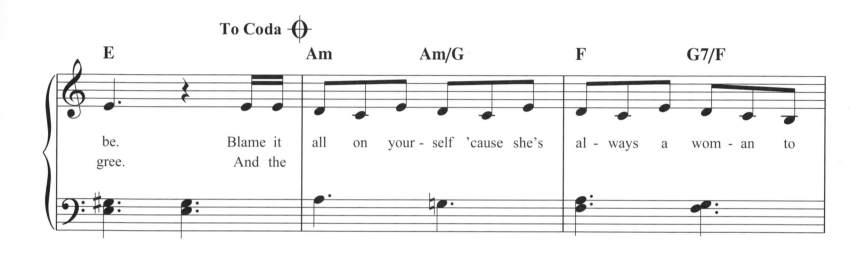

To Coda ⊕

E   **Am**   **Am/G**   **F**   **G7/F**

be. Blame it all on your - self 'cause she's al - ways a wom - an to
gree. And the

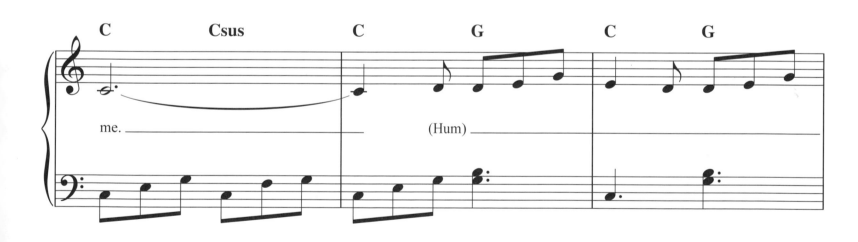

C   **Csus**   **C**   **G**   **C**   **G**

me. _____ (Hum) _____

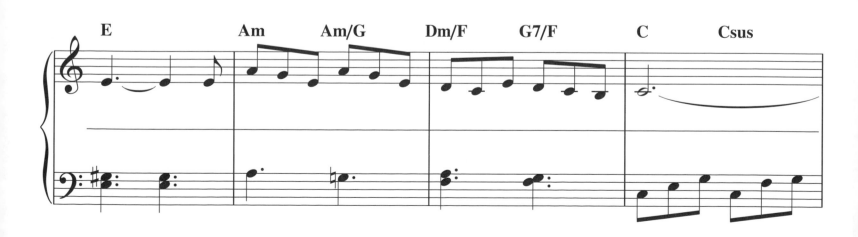

E   **Am**   **Am/G**   **Dm/F**   **G7/F**   **C**   **Csus**

STEPPIN' OUT

Words and Music by
JOE JACKSON

but nothing hides ___ the
We'll leave the T - V

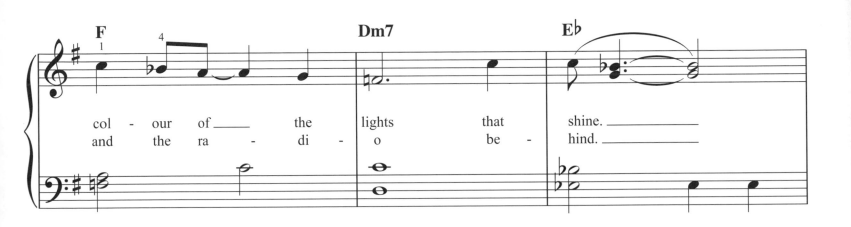

col - our of ___ the lights that shine. _____
and the ra - di - o be - hind. _____

E - lec - tric - i - ty so fine; _____
Don't you won - der what we'll find, _____

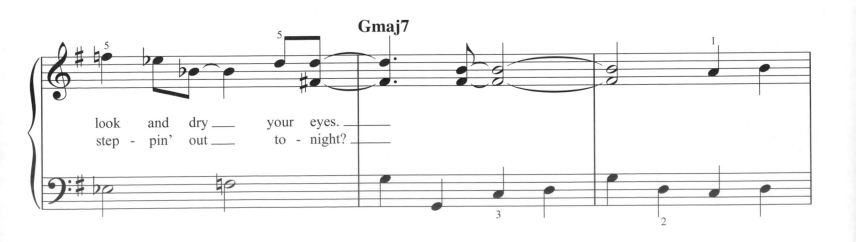

look and dry ___ your eyes. _____
step - pin' out ___ to - night? _____

We, _____
You _____

so tired of all ___ the darkness in our lives, ___
can dress in pink ___ and blue just like a child, ___

with no more an - gry
and in a yel - low

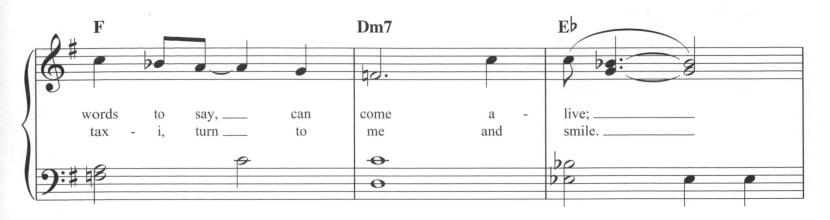

words to say, _____ can come a - live; _____
tax - i, turn _____ to me and smile. _____

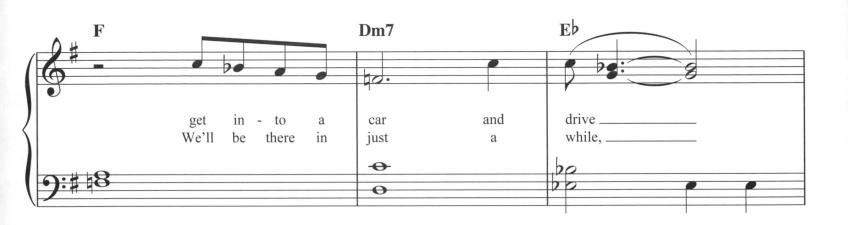

get in - to a car and drive _____
We'll be there in just a while, _____

to the oth - er side. _____
if you fol - low me. _____
Me, babe, _____ step - pin'

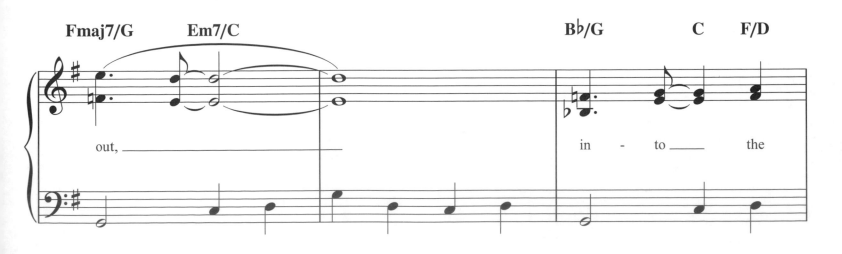

out, _____ in - to _____ the

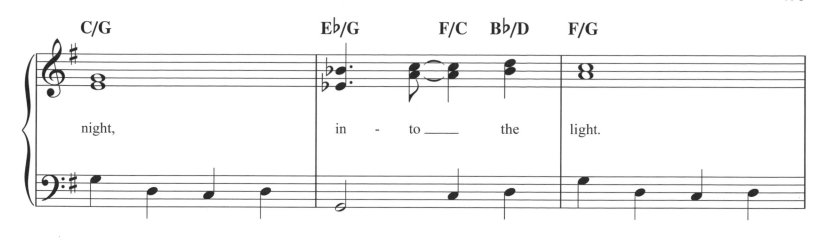

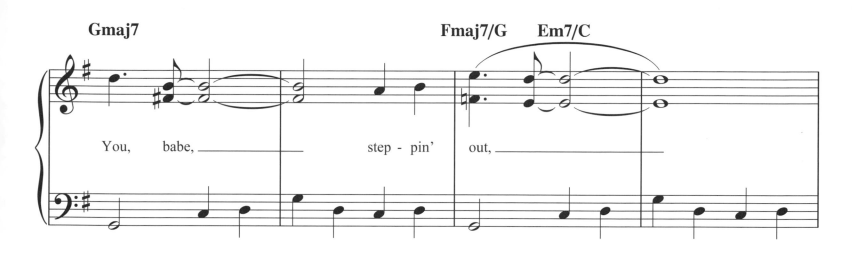

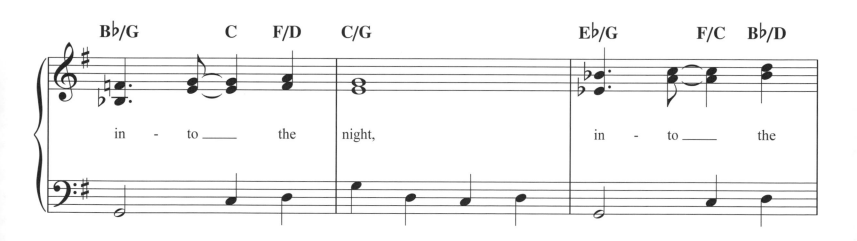

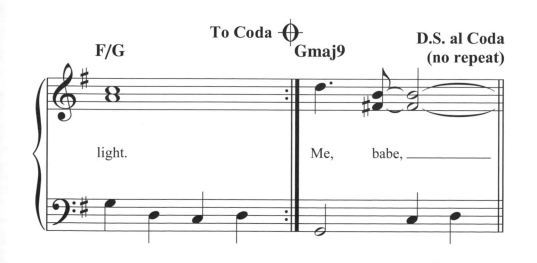

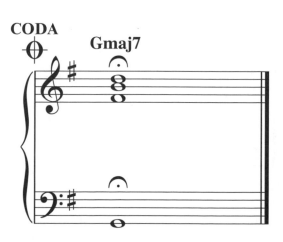

SHOW ME THE WAY

Words and Music by
PETER FRAMPTON

wonder how __ you're feel - ing. __
I can see __ no rea - son.

There's ring - ing in __ my ears, __
You're liv - ing on __ your nerves

The stars a - round ___ me shin - ing,
Well, some - one thought ___ of heal - ing, } but all I

real - ly want ___ to know: ___ Oh, won't you ___

show me the way, ev - 'ry day? ___ I want

you; ___ show me the way. ___

Well, way. Oh, _____ I want

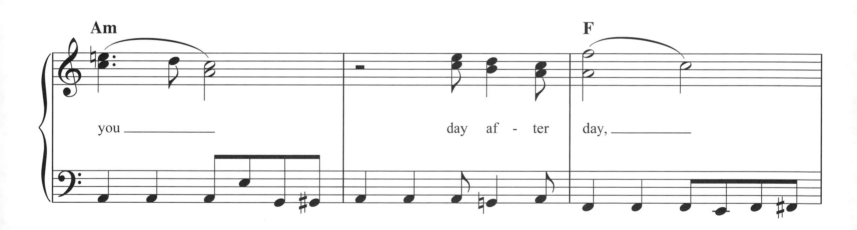

you _____ day af - ter day, _____

yeah. _____

I won-der if ___ I'm dream-ing.

___ I feel so un - a - shamed; ___ I

can't be - lieve ___ this is hap - pen - ing ___ to me. ___

I watch you when _ you're sleep - ing; well, then I _

_ want to take _ your love. ____ Oh, won't you _____

show me the way, ev - 'ry day? _____ I want

you; _____ show me the way. One more time! _

WE ARE THE CHAMPIONS

Words and Music by
FREDDIE MERCURY

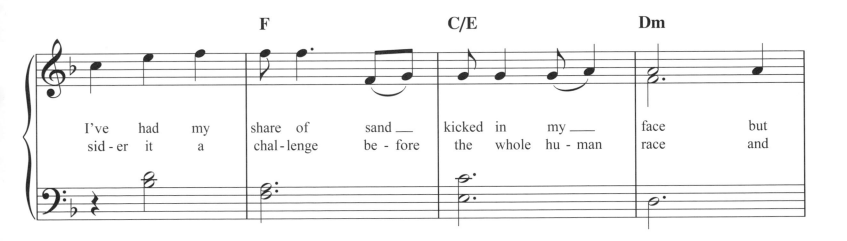

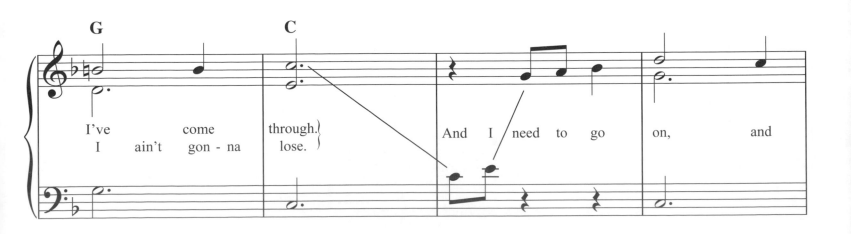

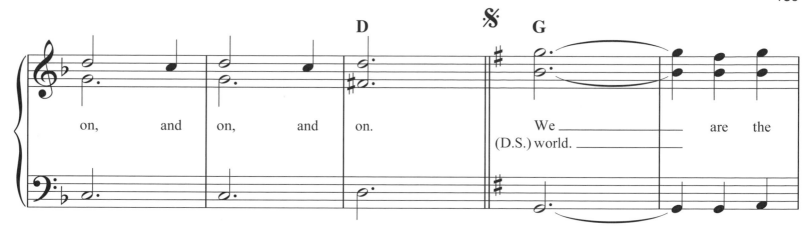

on, and on, and on.   We _____ are the
(D.S.) world. _____

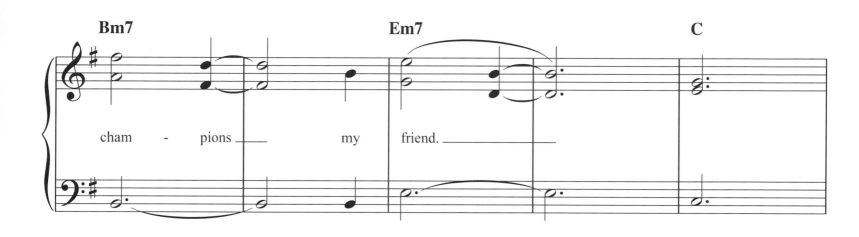

cham - pions _____ my friend. _____

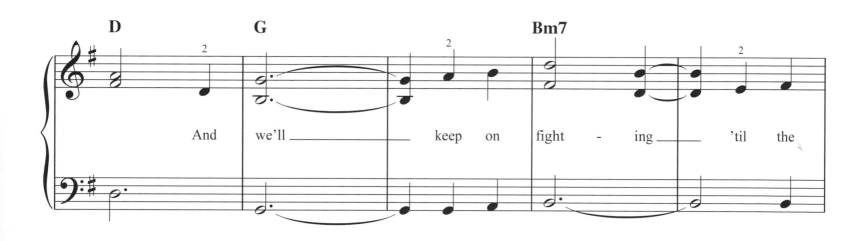

And   we'll _____ keep on fight - ing _____ 'til the

end. _____   We

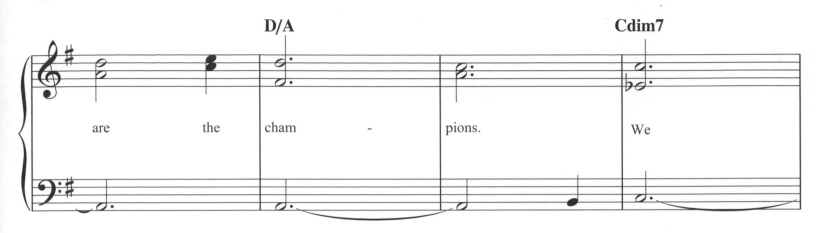

are   the   cham   -   pions.   We

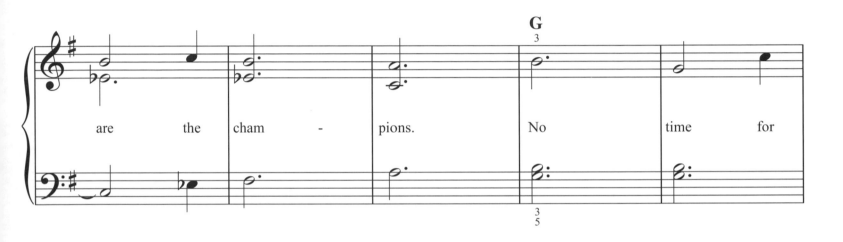

are   the   cham   -   pions.   No   time   for

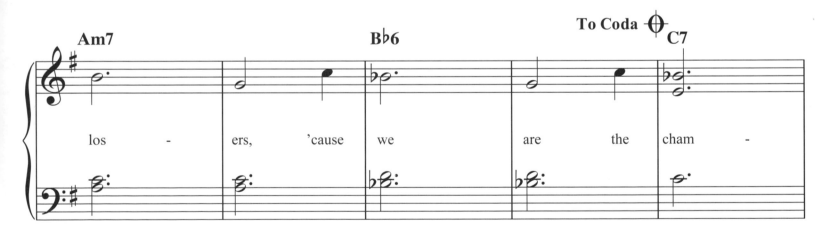

los   -   ers,   'cause   we   are   the   cham   -

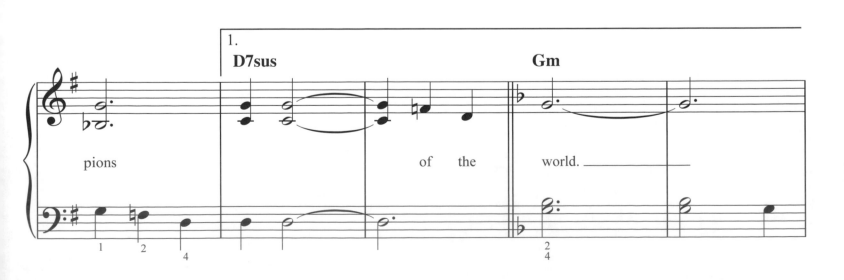

pions   of   the   world.

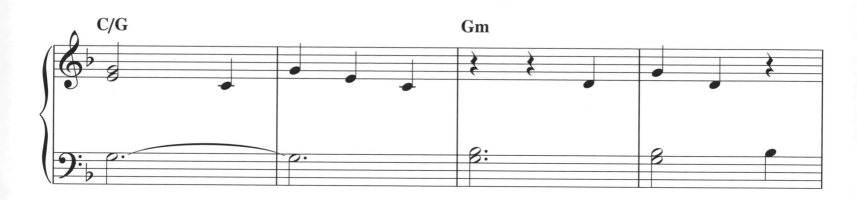

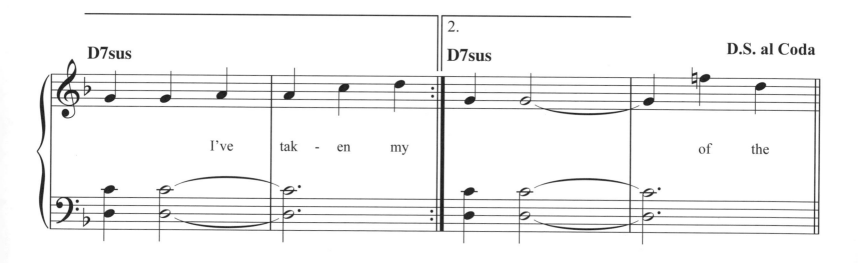

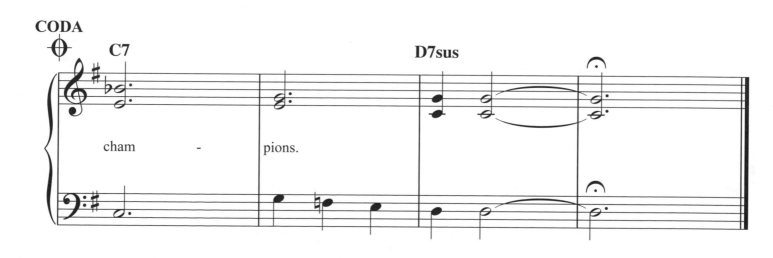

SISTER CHRISTIAN

Words and Music by
KELLY KEAGY

Moderate Rock

Sis - ter Chris - tian, oh, the
Babe, you know you're grow - ing

time has come. ___
up so fast. ___

And you know that you're ___ the
And Mom - ma's wor - ry - ing ___ that

on - ly one ___ to say ___ O. K. ___
you won't last ___ to say ___ let's play. ___

___
___
Where you go - ing, what ___ you
Sis - ter Chris - tian, there's ___ so

look - ing for? ___ You know those boys don't want ___ to
much in life. ___ Don't you give it up ___ be -

play no more with you. ___ It's true. ___
fore your time is due. ___ It's true. ___

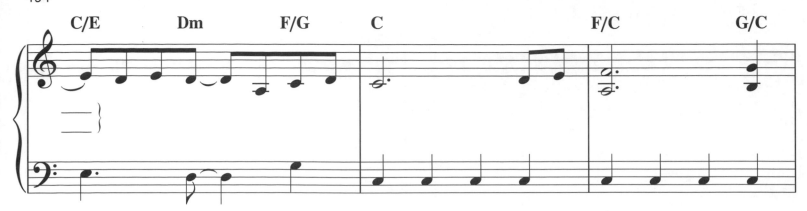

You're mo - tor - ing.

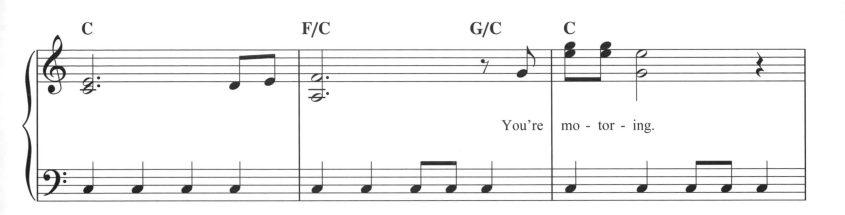

What's your price for flight? In

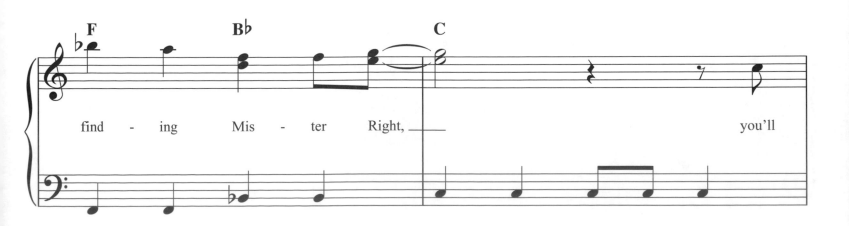

find - ing Mis - ter Right, you'll

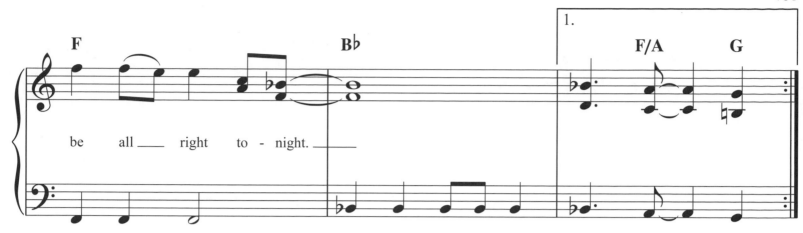

be all __ right to - night. __

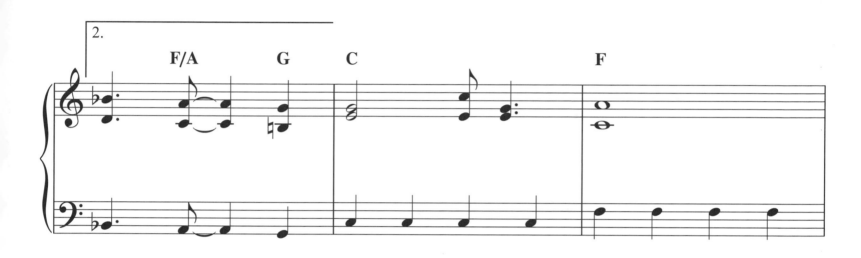

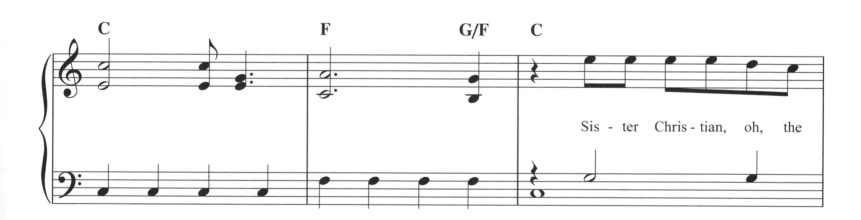

Sis - ter Chris - tian, oh, the

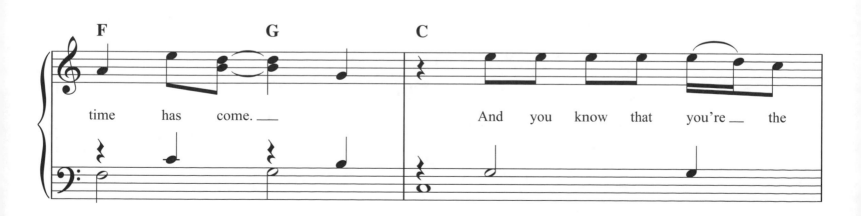

time has come. __ And you know that you're __ the

on - ly one _____ to say _____

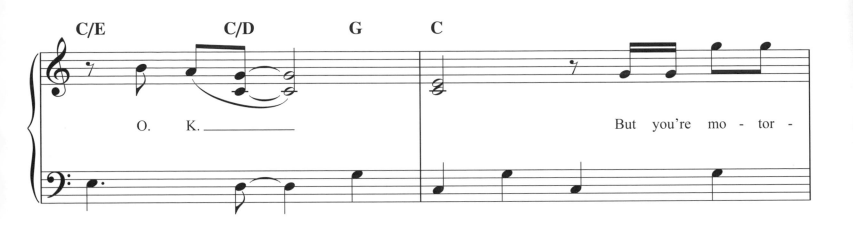

O. K. _____

But you're mo - tor -

ing. _____ You're _____ mo - tor -

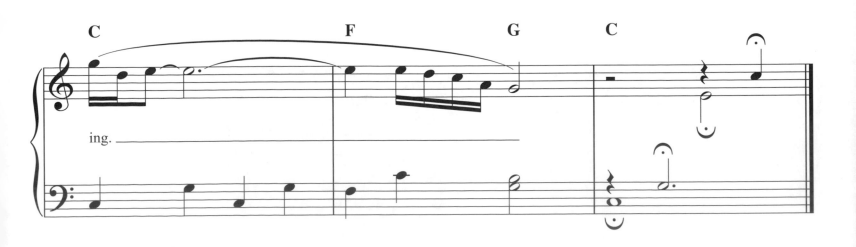

ing. _____

WEREWOLVES OF LONDON

Words and Music by WARREN ZEVON,
WADDY WACHTEL and LEROY MARINELL

Lee Ho Fooks ___ for to get a big dish of beef chow mein. ___

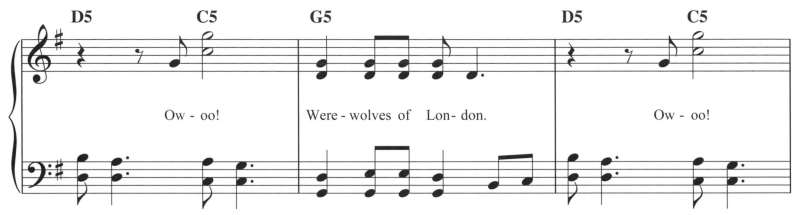

Ow - oo! Were - wolves of Lon - don. Ow - oo!

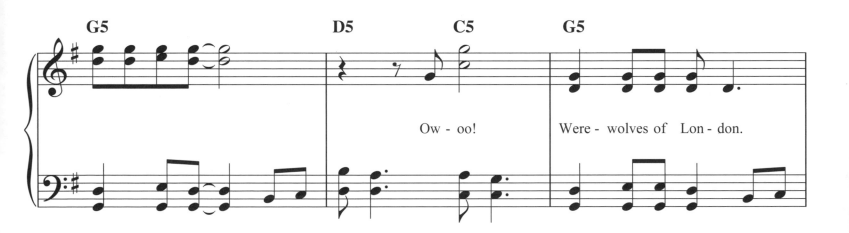

Ow - oo! Were - wolves of Lon - don.

Ow - oo! You hear him howl - in' a - round your

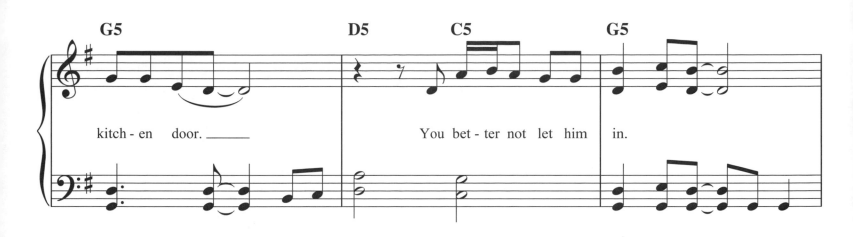

kitch - en door. _____ You bet - ter not let him in.

Lit - tle old la - dy got mu - ti - lat - ed late last night; ___

To Coda ⊕

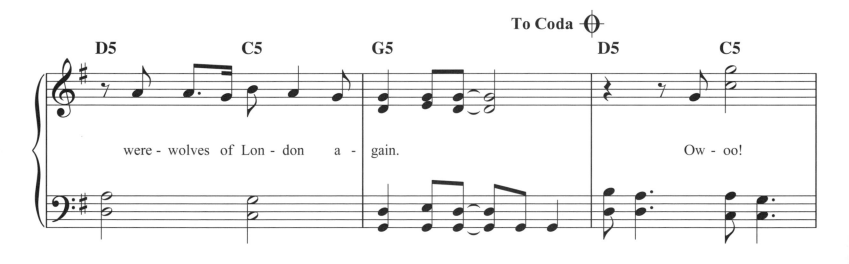

were - wolves of Lon - don a - gain. Ow - oo!

Were - wolves of Lon - don. Ow - oo!

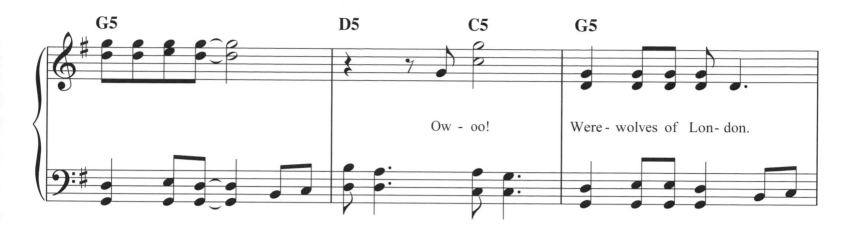

Additional Lyrics

He's the hairy-handed gent who ran amuck in Kent;
Lately, he's been overheard in Mayfair.
You better stay away from him!
He'll rip your lungs out, Jim!
Huh! I'd like to meet his tailor.

Ow-oo! Werewolves of London.
Ow-oo!
Ow-oo! Werewolves of London.
Ow-oo!

Well, I saw Lon Chaney walking with the Queen,
Doin' the Werewolves of London.
I saw Lon Chaney Junior walking with the Queen,
Doin' the Werewolves of London.

STILL THE SAME

Words and Music by
BOB SEGER

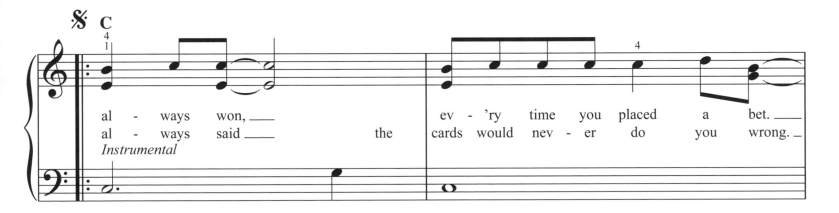

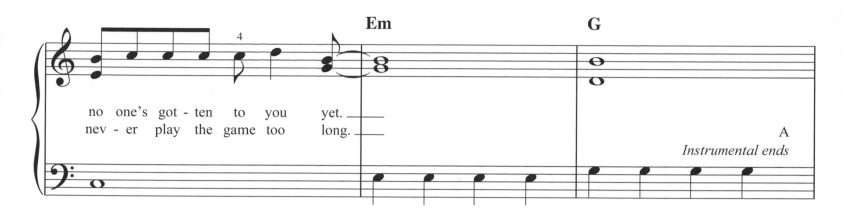

no one's got-ten to you yet. \
nev-er play the game too long.

Em **G**

Instrumental ends A

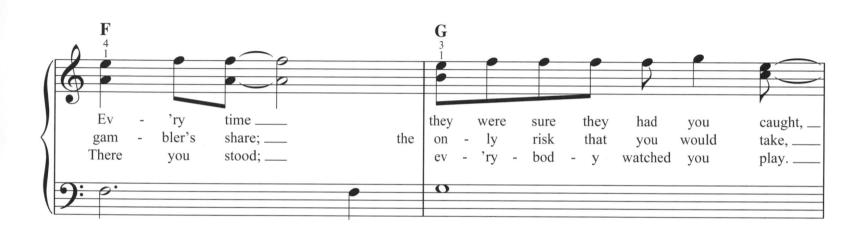

F **G**

Ev - 'ry time ____ the they were sure they had you caught, ___ \
gam - bler's share; ___ the on - ly risk that you would take, ___ \
There you stood; ___ ev - 'ry - bod - y watched you play. ___

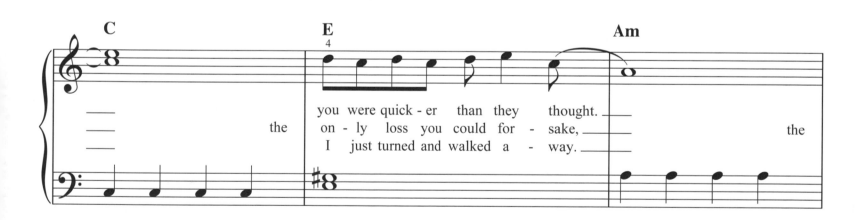

C **E** **Am**

___ the you were quick - er than they thought. ___ the \
___ on - ly loss you could for - sake, ___ \
___ I just turned and walked a - way. ___

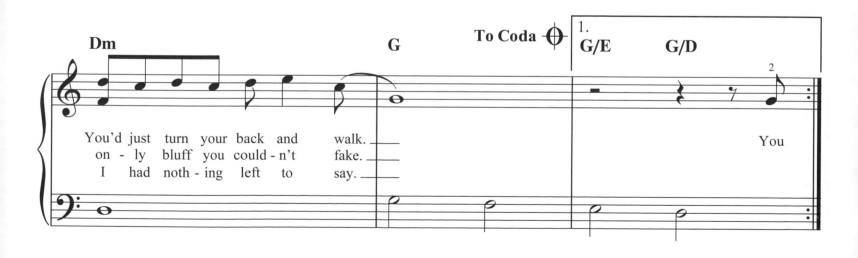

Dm **G** **To Coda** ⊕ **1.** **G/E** **G/D**

You'd just turn your back and walk. ___ \
on - ly bluff you could-n't fake. ___ \
I had noth - ing left to say. ___

You

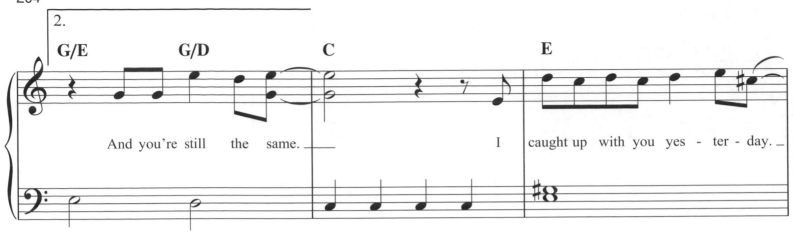

And you're still the same. I caught up with you yes - ter - day.

Mov - in' game to game;

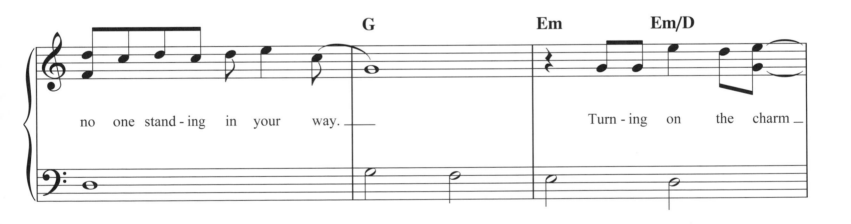

no one stand - ing in your way. Turn - ing on the charm

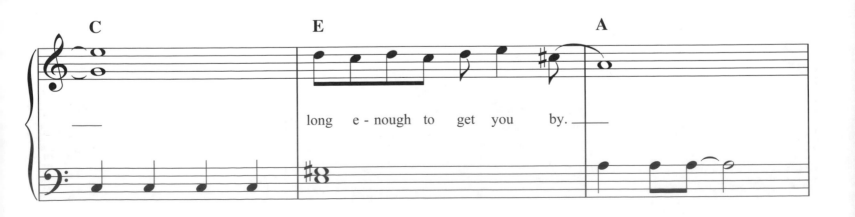

long e - nough to get you by.

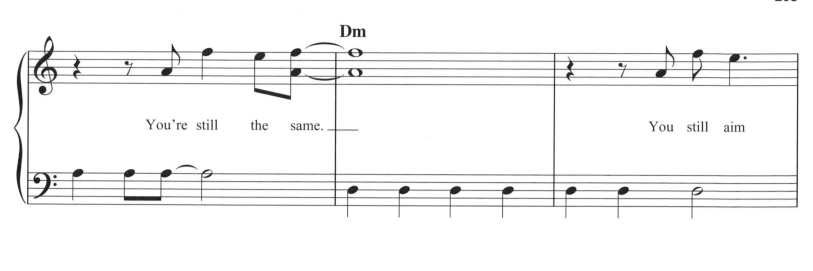

You're still the same. You still aim

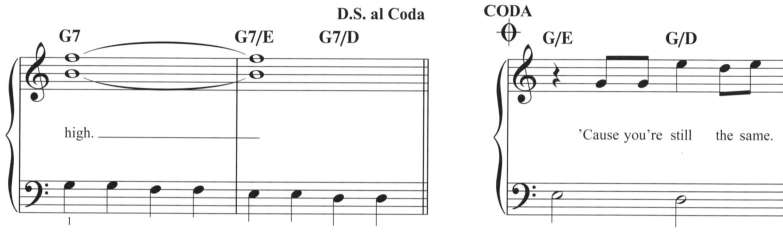

D.S. al Coda

CODA

G7 G7/E G7/D G/E G/D

high. 'Cause you're still the same.

C Em

1., 2. G

3. G C

Mov - ing game to game.
Some things nev - er change.

And you're still the same.

SWEET HOME ALABAMA

Words and Music by RONNIE VAN ZANT,
ED KING and GARY ROSSINGTON

Well, I heard Mis - ter Young sing a -

bout her.　　　　Well, I heard 'ole Neil ___ put her

down.　　　　Well, I hope Neil Young　　will re -

mem - ber.　　　A south - ern man don't need him a - round an - y - how.

Sweet home Al - a - bam - a, where the skies are so
blue, sweet home Al - a - bam - a,
Lord, I'm com - ing home to you.

To Coda ⊕

In Bir - ming - ham they love the
Now Mus - cle Shoals has got the

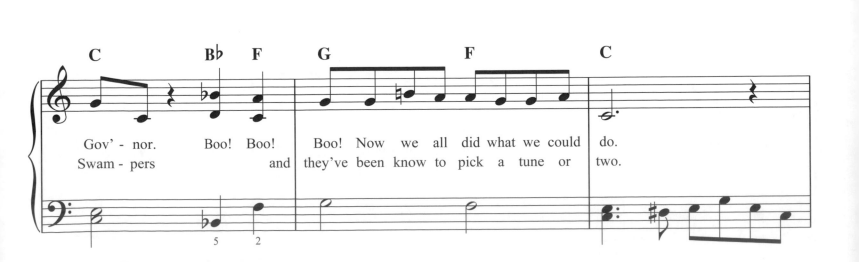

Gov' - nor. Boo! Boo! Boo! Now we all did what we could do.
Swam - pers and they've been know to pick a tune or two.

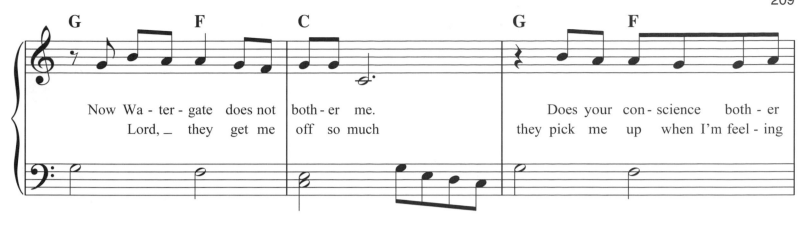

Now Wa - ter - gate does not both - er me.
Lord, _ they get me off so much

Does your con - science both - er
they pick me up when I'm feel - ing

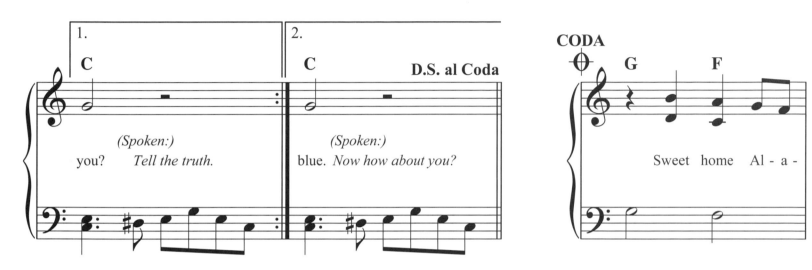

1.
(Spoken:)
you? *Tell the truth.*

2.
D.S. al Coda
(Spoken:)
blue. *Now how about you?*

CODA

Sweet home Al - a -

bam - a,

where the skies are so blue,

sweet home Al - a - bam - a,

Lord, I'm com - ing home to you.

THE WAY IT IS

Words and Music by
BRUCE HORNSBY

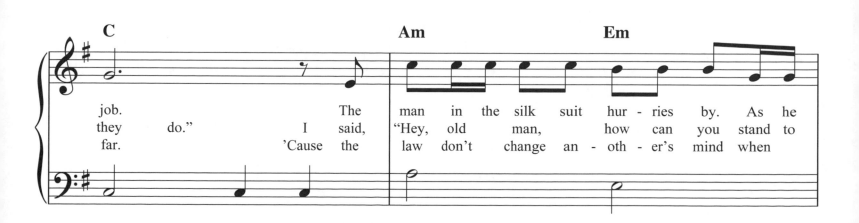

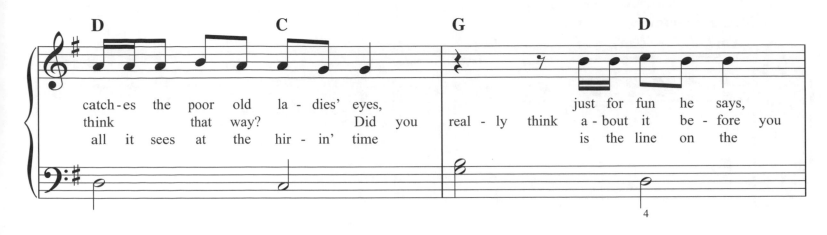

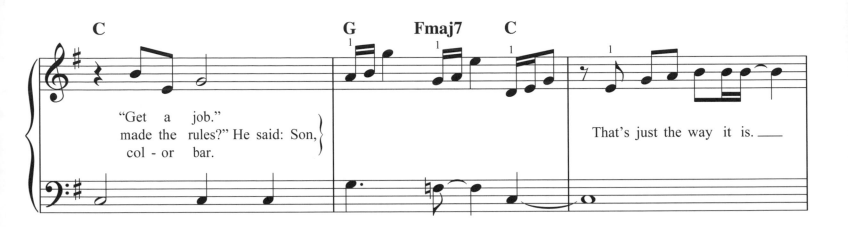

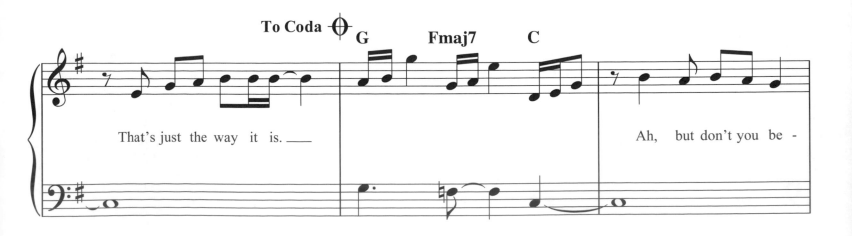

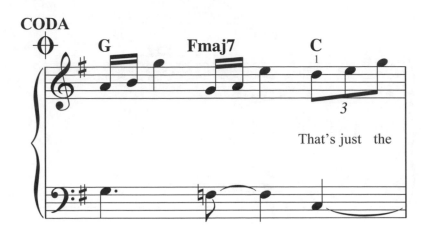

Well, they

That's just the

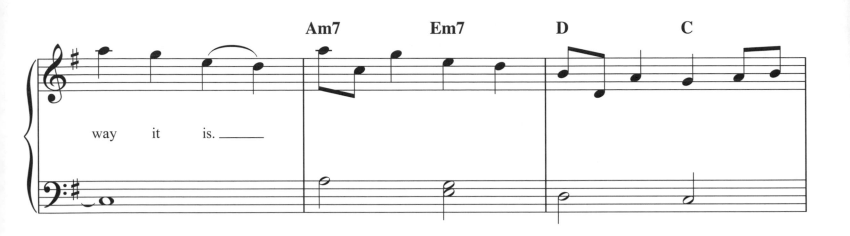

way it is. _____

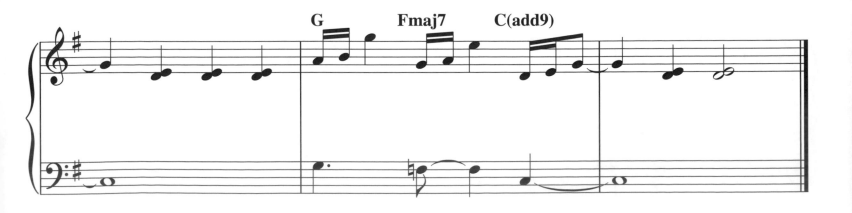

WHAT A FOOL BELIEVES

Words and Music by MICHAEL McDONALD
and KENNY LOGGINS

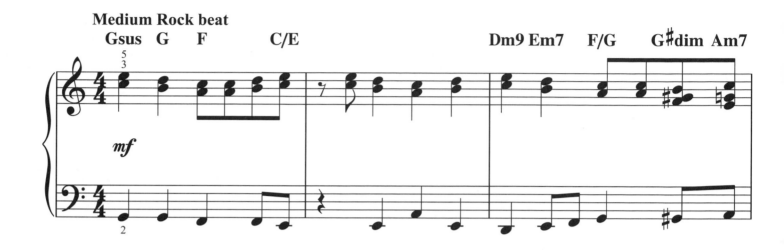

He came from some-where back in her long a-go, _____

the sen-ti-men-tal fool don't see, try-in' hard _____ to re-cre-ate what had

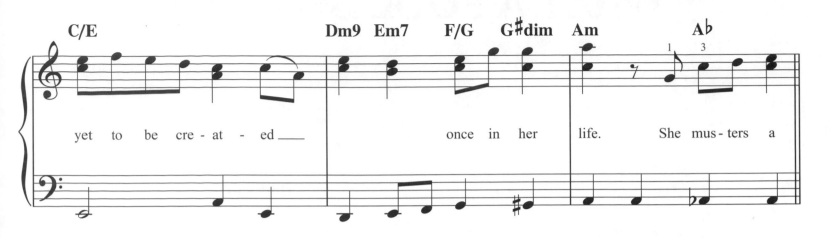

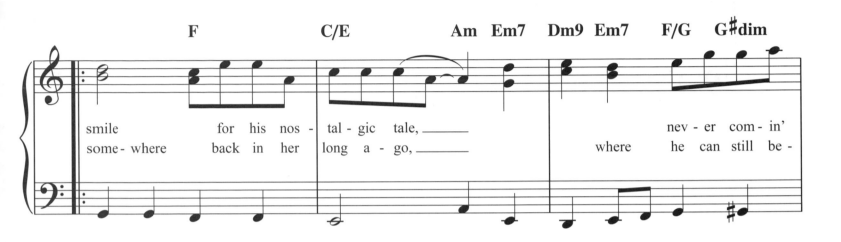

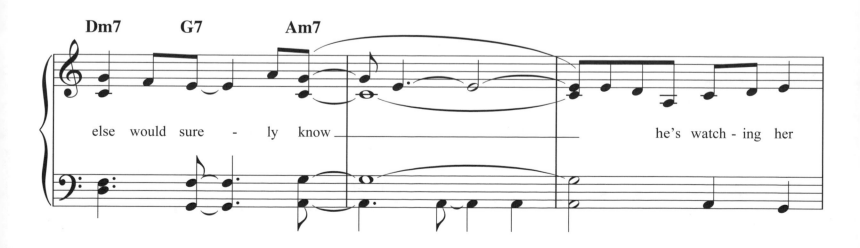

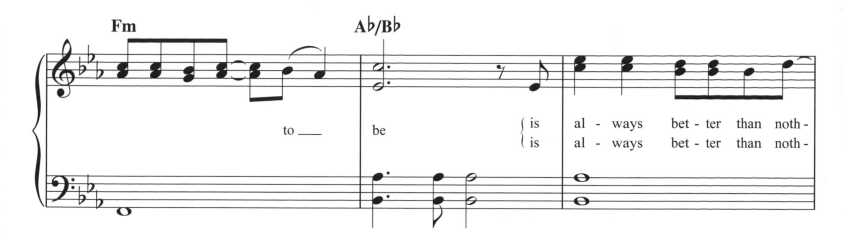

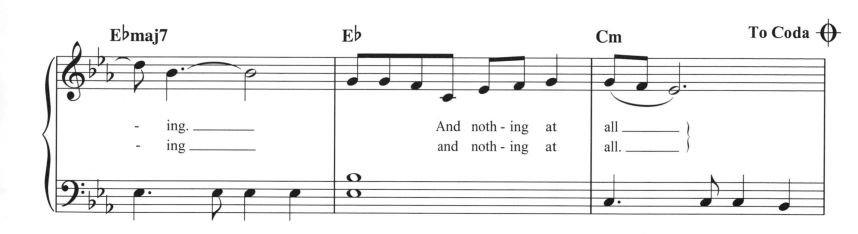

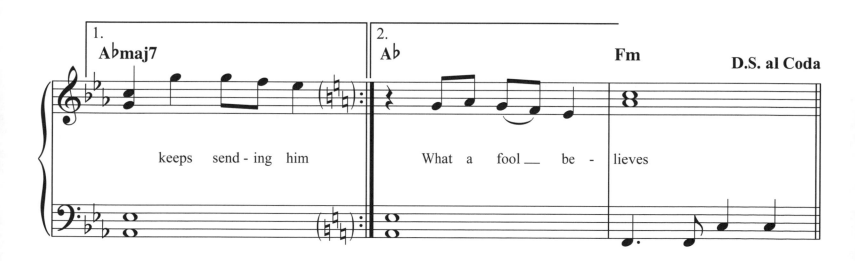

THE WEIGHT

By J.R. ROBERTSON

Moderately slow

1. I pulled in to Na-za-reth, ___ was feel-in' 'bout half-past dead.
2.–5. *(See additional lyrics)*

I just need some-place where I can lay my head. ___

"Hey, Mis-ter, can you tell me where a man might find a bed?"

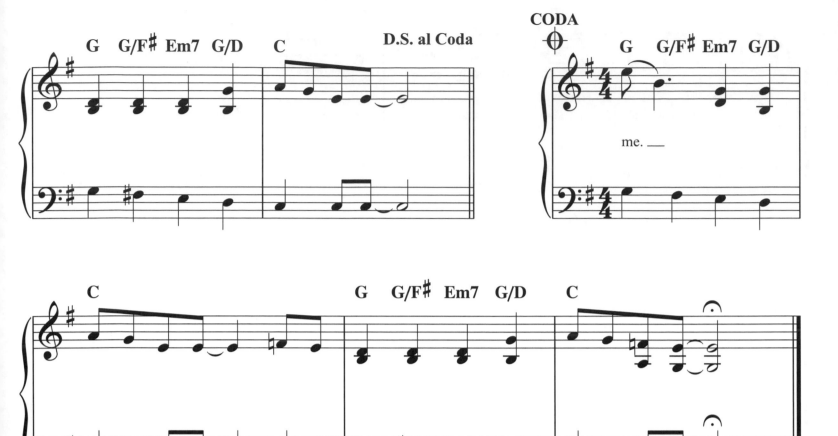

Additional Lyrics

2. I picked up my bag, I went looking for a place to hide,
   When I saw Carmen and the Devil walking side by side.
   I said, "Hey, Carmen, come on, let's go downtown."
   She said, "I gotta go but my friend can stick around."
   Chorus

3. Go down, Miss Moses, there's nothing you can say.
   It's just ol' Luke, and Luke's waiting on the judgement day.
   "Well, Luke, my friend, what about young Anna Lee?"
   He said, "Do me a favour, son, won't you stay
   And keep Anna Lee company?"
   Chorus

4. Crazy Chester caught me and followed me in the fog.
   He said, "I will fix your rack if you'll take Jack, my dog."
   I said, "Wait a minute, Chester, you know I'm a peaceful man."
   He said, "That's OK, boy, won't you feed him when you can?"
   Chorus

5. Catch a cannonball now, to take me down the line.
   My bag is sinking and I do believe it's time
   To get back to Miss Fanny, you know she's the only one
   Who sent me here with her regards for everyone.
   Chorus

WISH YOU WERE HERE

Words and Music by ROGER WATERS
and DAVID GILMOUR

Moderately slow, in 2

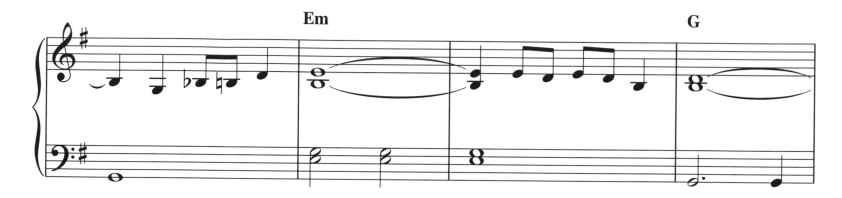

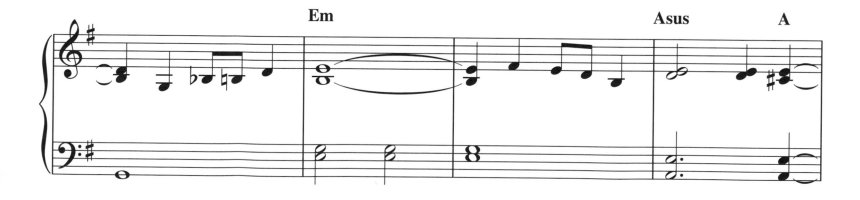

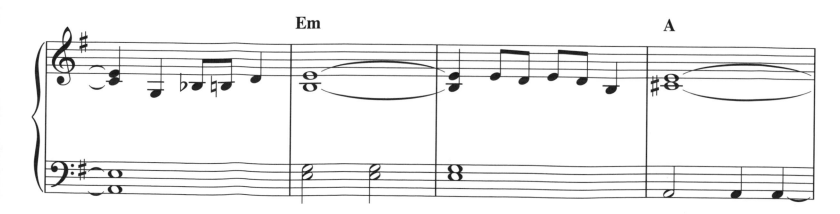

So, ____

so you think you can   tell _____   heav-en from   hell, ____

____ blue   skies __ from   pain. _____   Can you tell   a green   field _____

from a cold   steel   rail, _____   a   smile __ from a   veil?

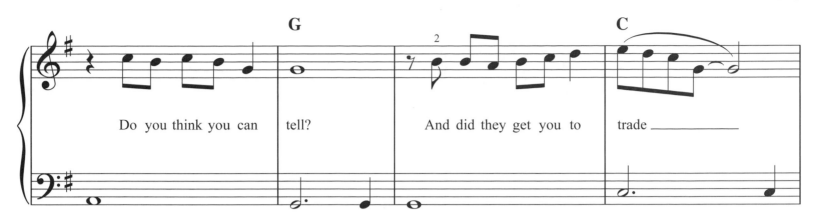

Do you think you can tell? And did they get you to trade _____

your he - roes for ghosts, ___ hot ash - es for trees, ___

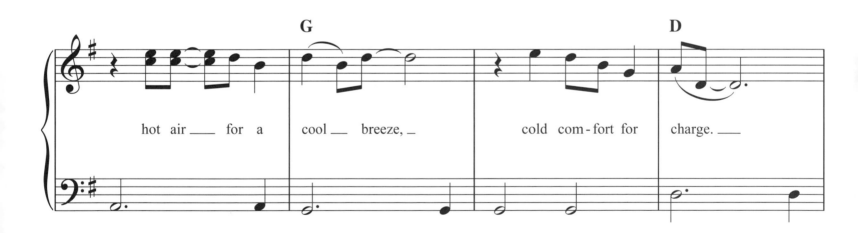

hot air ___ for a cool ___ breeze, ___ cold com-fort for charge. ___

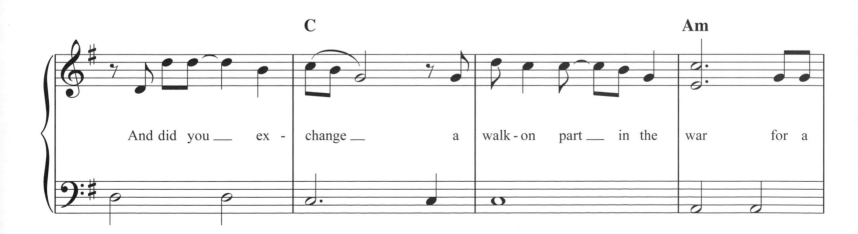

And did you ___ ex - change ___ a walk-on part ___ in the war for a

lead role ___ in a | cage? ___

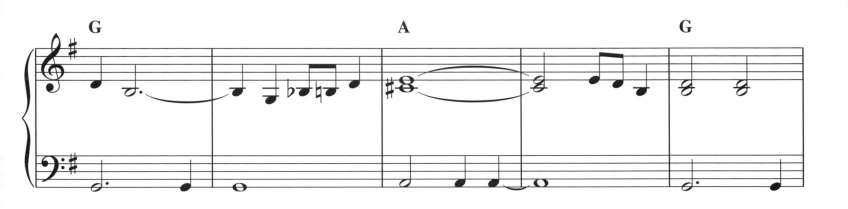

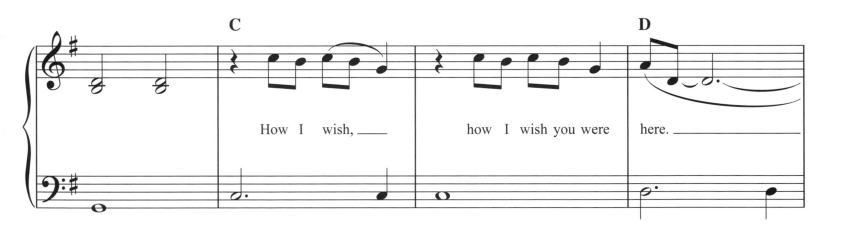

How I wish, ___ | how I wish you were | here. ___

___ | We're just | two lost souls swim-ming | in a fish - bowl. ___ | Year af - ter year, ___

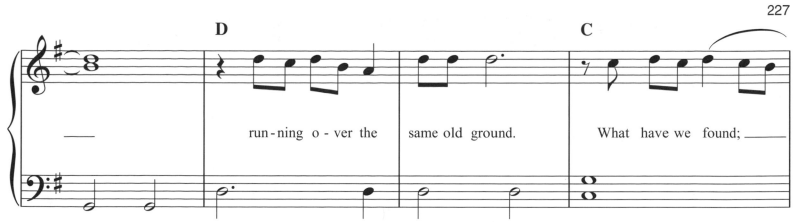

run-ning o - ver the   same old ground.   What have we found; _____

_____ the same old _____ fears. _____   Wish you _____ were _ here. _____

rit.

A WHITER SHADE OF PALE

Words and Music by KEITH REID,
GARY BROOKER and MATTHEW FISHER

1. We skipped the light fan-
2. She said, "I'm home on
3. *(See additional lyrics)*

dan - go, _____
shore leave," _____

turned cart - wheels 'cross the
though in truth we were at

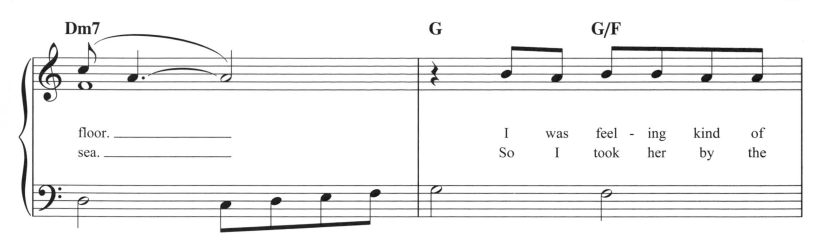

floor. _____
sea. _____

I was feel - ing kind of
So I took her by the

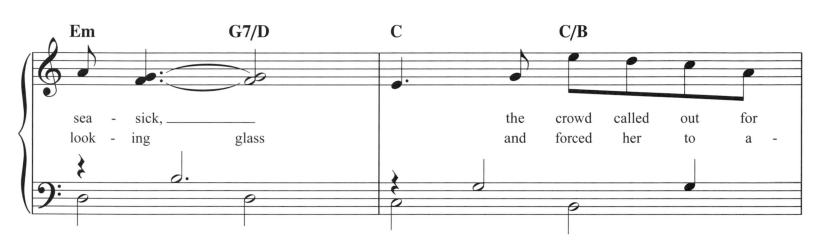

sea - sick, _____
look - ing glass

the crowd called out for
and forced her to a -

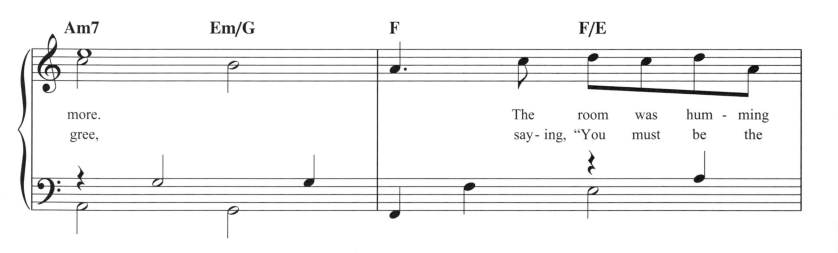

more.
gree,

The room was hum - ming
say - ing, "You must be the

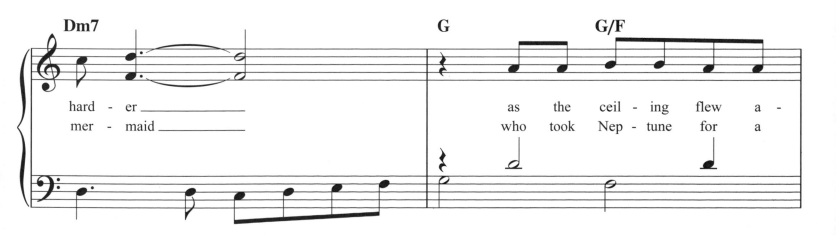

hard - er _____
mer - maid _____

as the ceil - ing flew a -
who took Nep - tune for a

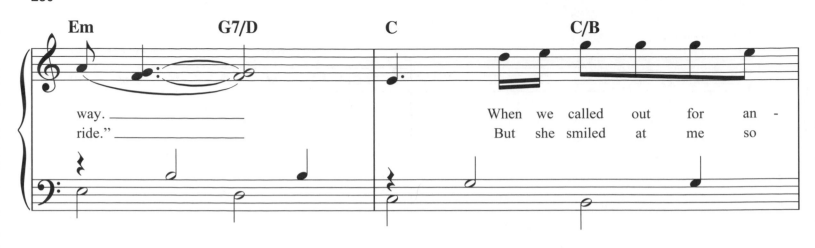

way. _____
ride." _____

When we called out for an -
But she smiled at me so

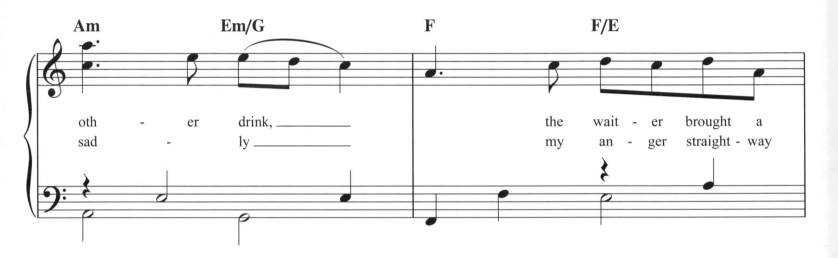

oth - er drink, _____
sad - ly _____

the wait - er brought a
my an - ger straight - way

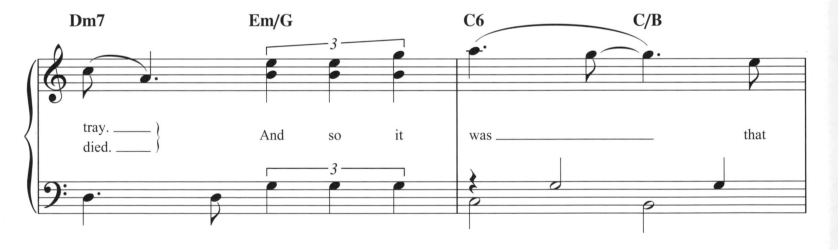

tray. ___ }
died. ___ }

And so it

was _____ that

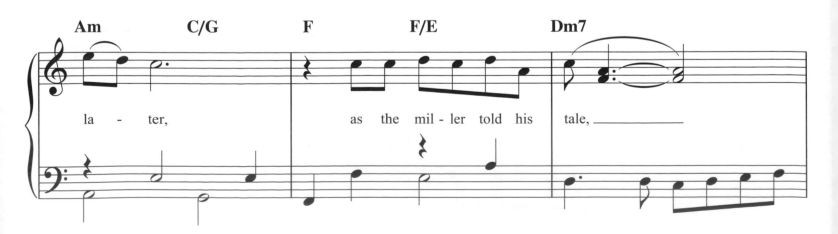

la - ter,

as the mil - ler told his

tale, _____

that her face, at first just ghost - ly, _____ turned a

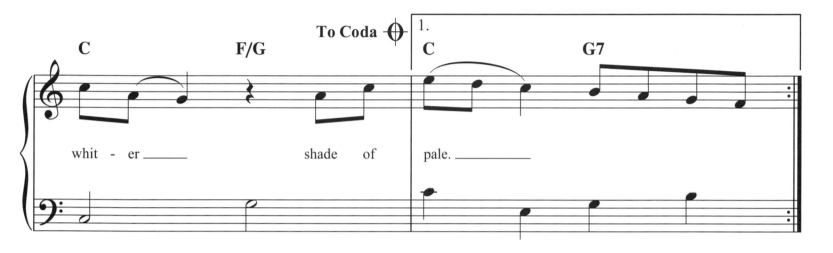

To Coda ⊕

1.

whit - er _____ shade of pale. _____

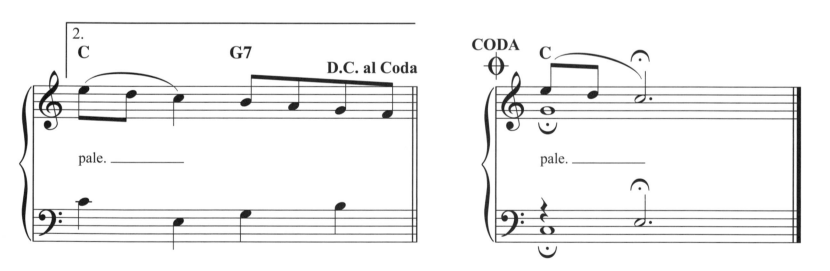

2.

D.C. al Coda

pale. _____

CODA ⊕

pale. _____

Additional Lyrics

3. She said, "There is no reason,
And the truth is plain to see."
But I wandered through my playing cards
And would not let her be
One of sixteen vestal virgins
Who were leaving for the coast.
And although my eyes were open,
They might just as well been closed.

WITHOUT YOU

Words and Music by PETER HAM
and THOMAS EVANS

No, I

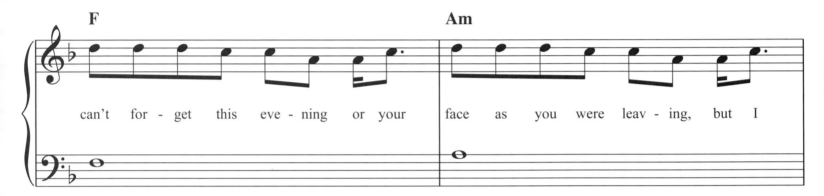

can't for-get this eve-ning or your face as you were leav-ing, but I

guess that's just the way the sto-ry goes. You al-ways

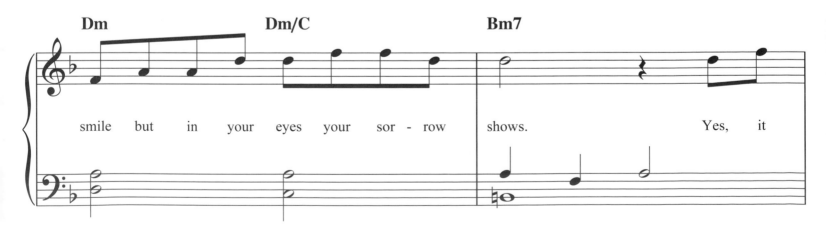

smile but in your eyes your sor-row shows. Yes, it

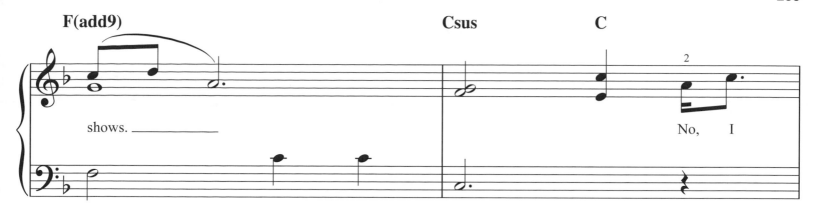

shows. _____

No, I

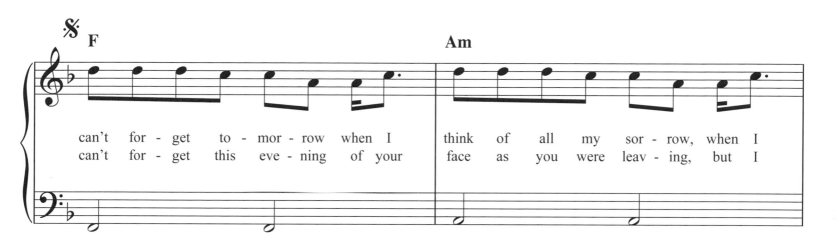

can't for - get to - mor - row when I
can't for - get this eve - ning of your

think of all my sor - row, when I
face as you were leav - ing, but I

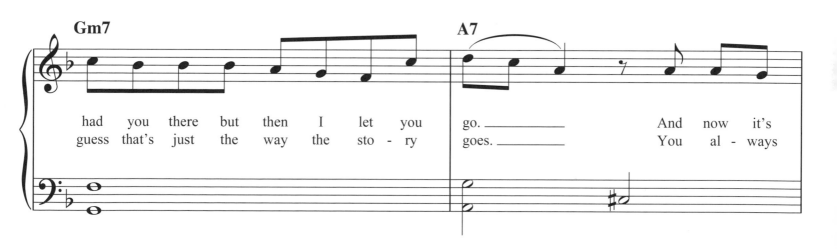

had you there but then I let you
guess that's just the way the sto - ry

go. _____ And now it's
goes. _____ You al - ways

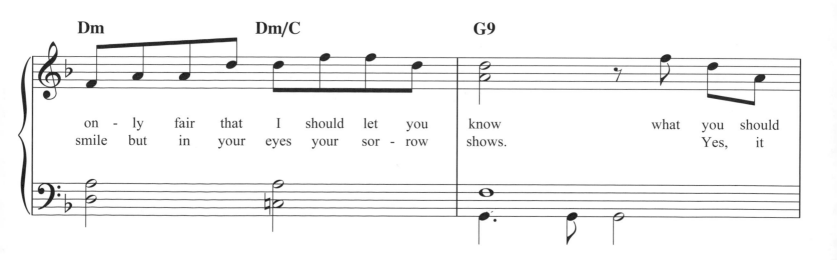

on - ly fair that I should let you
smile but in your eyes your sor - row

know _____ what you should
shows. Yes, it

To Coda ⊕

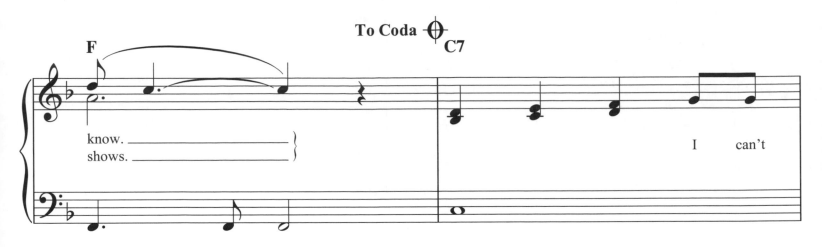

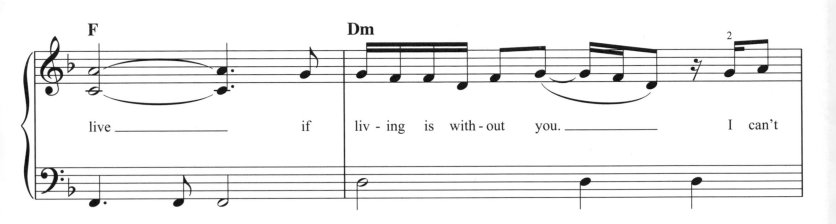

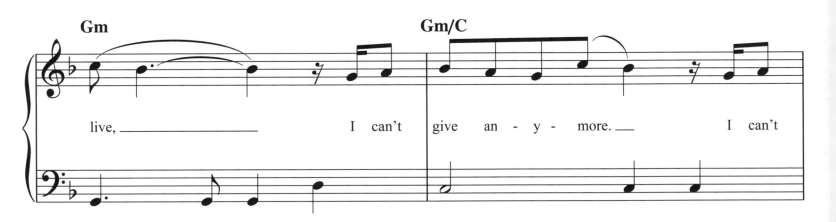

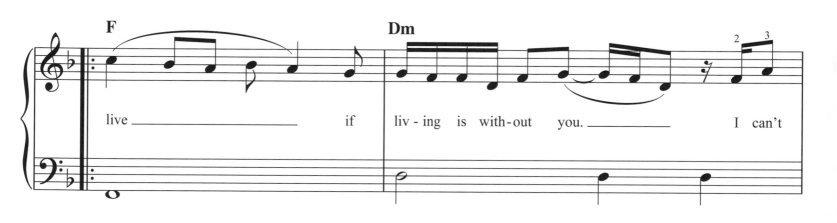

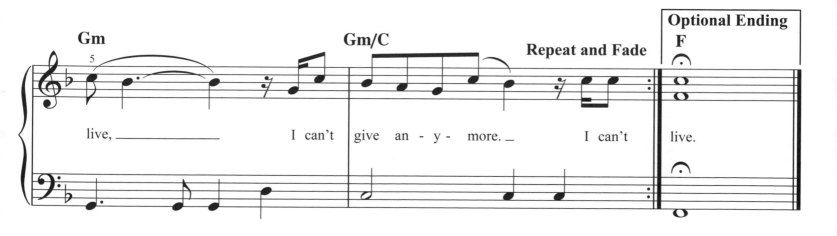

YOU CAN LEAVE YOUR HAT ON

Words and Music by
RANDY NEWMAN

Ba - by, take off your dress, ___ yes, yes, ___ yes. ___ You can

Cm7   **C7/E**   **F7**   **G7**

leave your hat on.   You can leave your hat on.   You can leave your hat

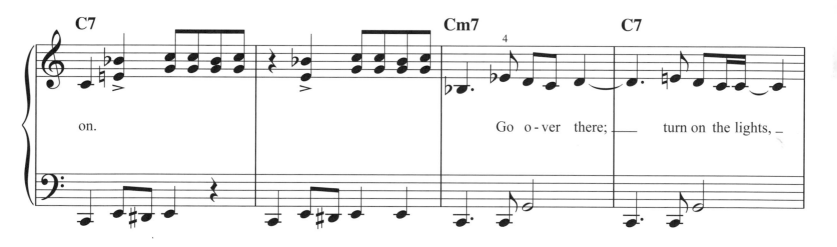

C7   **Cm7**   **C7**

on.   Go o - ver there; ___ turn on the lights, _

hey, all the lights.   Come o - ver here;   stand on that chair. _

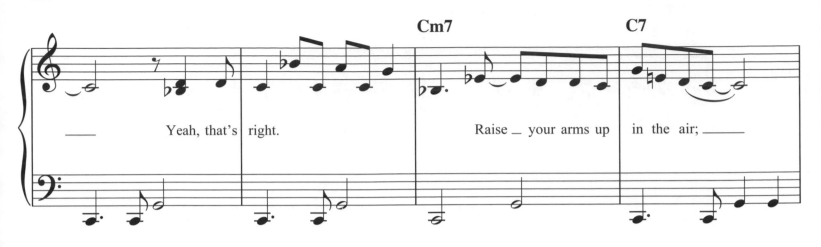

Yeah, that's right.   Raise — your arms up   in the air; ___

now shake ___ 'em.   Now give me rea-son to live.   You give me rea-son to live.

You give me rea-son to live.   You give me rea-son to   live. ___   Sweet

dar-ling,   you can leave your hat   on.   You can   leave your hat on.

They don't know what love is.   They don't

know _ what love is.   But I know what love is.

You can leave your hat on.